CONSERVATISM IN EARLY AMERICAN HISTORY

LEONARD WOODS LABAREE

Cornell Paperbacks

CORNELL UNIVERSITY PRESS

ITHACA AND LONDON

CORNELL UNIVERSITY PRESS

First printing, Great Seal Books, 1959
Second printing, 1962
Third printing, Cornell Paperbacks, 1965
Fourth printing, 1967
Fifth printing, 1968
Sixth printing, 1972

Published in the United Kingdom by Cornell University Press Ltd.,
2-4 Brook Street, London W1Y 1AA

International Standard Book Number 0-8014-9008-1

PRINTED IN THE UNITED STATES OF AMERICA
BY VALLEY OFFSET, INC.

FOREWORD

One of the persistent influences in Western civilization has been the phenomenon we call "conservatism." Like those other forces known as "liberalism" and "radicalism," it has played and continues to play a significant part in the development of society and the shaping of events. This volume undertakes to examine the conservative elements in one segment of that civilization, the English-speaking colonies of North America, and in a limited period of history, the century before the attainment of independence. It is offered in the hope that it may contribute, in a small degree, to an understanding of one of the important influences both in the early formative period of American history and in our present-day society.

These lectures are printed substantially as they were delivered during the spring of 1947. Footnotes have been introduced and some paragraphs added to the text which the limitations of time did not permit me to include in the oral presentation. I have made a few verbal changes for purposes of publication and have reversed the order of the first two lectures. Otherwise, the work stands essentially unchanged and remains, as it was written, a series of lectures, not a monographic study. In all quotations, spelling, capitalization, and punctuation have been modernized.

Part of the material in two lectures is drawn from articles previously printed. I am grateful to the editors of the *William and Mary Quarterly* for permission to include in the last part of the third lecture some passages from an essay on "The Conservative Attitude Toward the Great Awakening," published in the October 1944 issue of that journal, and to the American Antiquarian Society for authority to reproduce in the final lecture scattered portions of my paper on "The Nature of American Loyalism" from its *Proceedings* for April 1944. Miss Janet Zimmerman, who has twice typed the complete manuscript, deserves my warmest thanks for her patience and painstaking care. Lastly, I would express my appreciation to the Chancellor's Committee on the Phelps Lectures of New York University for the invitation to deliver these lectures and to the members of the University for their co-operation and hospitality.

L. W. L.

New Haven, Connecticut
May 21, 1947

CONTENTS

INTRODUCTION

The hundred years ending with the achievement of independence was a period of enormous change in the pattern of American life. Even the casual student of that century will note the vast expansion of the population and of the area of actual settlement; he will remark the arrival of large numbers of Continental Europeans and Scotch-Irish as well as of thousands of unwilling immigrants from Africa and will see how greatly they modified the predominantly English character of the original racial stock.

Other less easily noticed developments took place in American culture. There was, for example, the beginning of a political and social philosophy that, in time, was to grow into the nineteenth-century concept of democracy. The religious outlook likewise underwent a profound change. New England Puritanism, already past its pristine vigor in the 1680's, lost much more of its vitality during the next hundred years, while throughout the land there appeared new sects like Methodism, fresh menaces to orthodoxy like Arminianism, and new philosophies like deism. There was a weakening of the bond between church and state, which, if it did not achieve complete disestablishment everywhere in America, at least brought wider toleration and a greater extension of religious liberty. During this hundred years the American people underwent not just one revolution, but many, affecting every phase of life and culture.

The forces that brought about these changes were numerous

and most of them are familiar. The new elements in the population carried over with them new cultural patterns, and generations of native-born Americans arose to whom the European background was merely a tradition and not a personal experience. Climate and topography forced changes and adaptations in the economic and social structure. New ideas drifted in from across the seas, took root, and flourished mightily in the fresh American soil. Facilities for the easier interchange of information and ideas developed, such as towns, highways, and newspapers. The sheer weight of experience fostered political self-consciousness and social maturity, and the frontier was ever present as a liberalizing influence. In the English-speaking colonies of the North American continent, forces of change were vigorously and openly in action in the eighteenth century, working with ever-increasing momentum.

These forces operated in an environment that added to their effectiveness. Physical separation from the older centers of Western culture, relative freedom from external political control, and a people whose very presence in the colonies was evidence that they or their forefathers had welcomed change of one sort or another created conditions that fostered the developments taking place. So suitable, in fact, were the environment and the population that the basic question might well be not why did change take place so rapidly and so extensively but rather why did it fail to go on at an even faster rate or carry to a greater distance.

The answer lies in the fact that there were other forces and influences at work, less powerful than those leading to change, but still strong enough to retard the velocity of the transformation, and, in some degree at least, to alter its direction. Some significant facts come readily to mind. The colonists were, after all, Europeans — and still mostly of English stock — men and women who, until the achievement of independence, tended to look upon the mother country as "home," and who took no little pride in their connections with Europe. In spite of the degree of political autonomy which the English colonies enjoyed, in all but two of them governmental executives and many administrative officials were appointed from England, while local legislation and the more important judicial decisions were subject to review and approval there. In matters of trade as well as of military and naval protection the colonies were largely dependent on the resources of Great Britain, and in both respects gained advantages from the connection. Furthermore, in spite of the people's receptivity to change, they were still men of their age, circumscribed by its points of view, limited by its traditions, trained in its habits of mind. Many there were ready and able to move in the vanguard of thought and action; but there were others, often among the most prominent and influential, who clung tenaciously to the old and the accustomed, either from natural inclination or from interest, and who did what they could to resist the forces of change.

If we are to have a clear understanding of the true course of American life during the century which ended with independence, it is necessary that we examine not only the men and ideas working to transform American society but also those tending to retard that change. To put it concretely, we must understand not only such influences as frontier liberalism and such men as the Revolutionary radicals but also such forces as royal government and Puritan orthodoxy, such groups as the planter aristocrats and the seaport merchants, and such men as the Anglican clergy and the Revolutionary Loyalists. Only by taking note of the conservative side of colonial thought and action, as well as the liberal, can we arrive at a true estimate of the whole.

It is my purpose, therefore, to inquire into the nature of conservatism in early American history. We shall examine the characteristics and attitudes of some of the groups of people who tended to resist change in the pattern of life and whose influence, whether consciously or unconsciously directed, was exerted against the modifying forces of new ideas and the new environment.

Just what do I mean by "conservative"? Like all abstractions, the word defies exact and all-inclusive definition. Something of what I mean by the term will be apparent from what I have already said. In general, I use it to describe the attitude of a person who tends to support the existing state of affairs in respect to any particular aspect of social relationships in opposition to efforts toward modification. Conservatism, as here used, is an attitude of mind that tends to promote resistance to change. It is not an absolute but a variable. It may be present in different individuals in differing degrees: on any issue there may be conservatives so moderate as to be practically indistinguishable from the more cautious liberals on the other side; on the same issue there may be conservatives so extreme that they border on the reactionary. Again, although a conservative attitude tends to be a consistent habit of mind, it is altogether possible for a man to be a decided conservative in one relation of life but a liberal or even an out-and-out radical in another. Jonathan Trumbull, for example, was a stanch supporter of the conservative "standing order" in the religious and social system of colonial Connecticut and a man who was bitterly criticized after the Revolution for upholding the privileges of the officer class in the American Army, yet he was the one colonial governor who repudiated his oath of allegiance to the British Crown and engaged in open rebellion.

Conservatism is not the monopoly of any one group of people; it manifests itself at all levels of society. Yet it is a common observation that a conservative attitude is most pronounced among the economically and socially privileged. Those who, through birth or their own efforts, are in the most favored position are usually the ones who risk the biggest loss from any impending change. Furthermore, in the period with which we are to deal, these were, among conservatives, generally the people with the best education and hence the ones most likely to commit their thoughts to paper and so leave an enduring record of their attitude for the edification of future generations. Almost inevitably, therefore, we shall draw our illustrations of colonial conservatism largely from the words and actions of the men of wealth and of social and political standing in the community. It must be remembered, however, that there were many lesser men who agreed with them on the issues of the day, but who, leaving no personal record, have passed on into that great majority, the forgotten men of history.

Conservatism, then, as we shall use the term, means an attitude of resistance to change shown in varying degrees by a variety of people with reference to any issue of the day. In the nature of the subject immediately before us, I shall use the term with particular regard to the political, economic, religious, and social conditions in the American colonies during the century before the Declaration of Independence. It is in reference to these matters that we shall consider some of the features of American conservatism.

RULING FAMILIES

One of the self-evident truths of human society, declares a famous document of 1776, is "that all men are created equal." Thomas Jefferson doubtless believed the statement when he wrote it, and the other signers may have been equally sincere when they pledged to its support their lives, their fortunes, and their sacred honor. Nevertheless, the principle of human equality was almost as revolutionary a concept in the world at large, when it was set forth in the Declaration, as the independence from Great Britain which the document was chiefly intended to proclaim and justify. Yet the very fact that Jefferson deemed it prudent to include his famous generalization in a state paper written with "a decent respect to the opinions of mankind" suggests that the notion of equality did command some support among the people of his day. The trend toward something which ultimately became nineteenth-century political democracy was without question one of the most significant developments of the colonial period.

Political equality, however—to say nothing of any other kind of equality—was far from being attained during the colonial period. Putting the matter in its most elementary terms, we need remind ourselves only that property qualifications for the right to vote existed everywhere at the time of the Revolution and that even higher qualifications were often imposed upon those who would represent their fellows in public office. While political privileges were undoubtedly more widely distributed in the English colonies than in almost any other part of the world, they were far from universal, and they rested primarily upon an economic base. And when one has called attention to that well-known fact, one has mentioned only a part of what needs to be understood. Even within the limits of the property qualifications, the male inhabitants were far from equal in their ability to exercise actual political power. There was, in fact, in almost every colony a definite ruling class. This class not only dominated the local political machinery, filled all or nearly all the important local offices, and spoke on public matters in behalf of all, but it also used its power very largely for the benefit of its own members, often at the expense of other less privileged parts of the community, and exerted all its efforts, throughout the period, to prevent the development of a more democratic system. The colonial ruling class was unquestionably one of the most important forces of conservatism in the colonies.

In some colonies, such as Massachusetts, a ruling group had been present from the start; in others, such as North Carolina, the process had taken a little longer. But by 1700 there was no colony, with the possible exception of Rhode Island, in which certain men had not attained a degree of wealth or position, usually both, which gave them a substantial measure of authority over their fellow colonists. Some of these leaders could point with pride to an aristocratic background or connection in England as an explanation of their position in America; others owed their rise to thrift, hard work, and foresight, or to sheer native ability; still others had taken advantage of opportunities to acquire land or other forms of wealth by methods that do not always bear too close inspection. Whatever the origin of such men's positions, however they came to the top, they tried to stay there themselves and to pass on to their children the standing in colonial society which they had achieved.

Very soon there came into being groups of leading families,

made up of the men of wealth and position, their children, and their children's children. It was inevitable that such families should intermarry, and so they did, not just occasionally, but repeatedly, until in some cases, notably in Virginia and New York, their genealogical trees became veritable jungles of interwoven branches, the despair of the researcher, but the pride of their descendants. Thus was built up, largely within each colony, but with interconnections across provincial lines, a substantial group of families whose members considered themselves, and who were generally considered by their fellow colonists, to represent the "upper crust" in America.

For the most part, these groups included in each colony the men of greatest wealth. Among them in the South were the great planters; in the Middle Colonies, the large landholders of Pennsylvania and New York and the principal proprietors of New Jersey. In these colonies, as well as in New England, the chief merchants of the seaport towns and the leading lawyers and other professional men usually became affiliated with the dominant groups. In New England the occupational foundation of leadership was not quite so clearly defined as elsewhere, partly because wealth was more evenly distributed, especially in the case of land, than in most of the other colonies. Many of the upper circle in Massachusetts and Connecticut were men of substance, but religious orthodoxy, even as late as the Revolution, education, and other personal characteristics more often played a role in the attainment and retention of leadership there than in some of the other colonies.

In contrast to most present-day leaders of "Society" these colonial individuals and families took a prominent part in political affairs. It was they above all others who held the responsible and lucrative offices. Judges, sheriffs, naval officers, provincial secretaries, and treasurers, for example, were almost always appointed from among the colonial "gentlemen." It was such men who, in the latter years of the seventeenth century and the first part of the eighteenth, were the leaders in the provincial assemblies. As time went on and the heads of these families reached greater heights than that of election to the popular branch of the assembly, it was still they who, to a marked extent, controlled the elections from behind the scenes, much as in contemporary England the great Whig landed families, whose heads sat in the House of Lords, controlled elections to the Commons. It was these provincial leaders, furthermore, who occupied almost exclusively the seats on the colonial councils. The important offices were reserved for those whom Governor Shute of Massachusetts once described as "most distinguished for their wealth, understanding, and probity."[1]

If we are to get a clear picture of these groups and of the extent to which they dominated colonial politics, we can approach the subject most easily by an examination of the colonial councils which they monopolized. Membership in the council is admittedly a rather artificial or arbitrary basis for studying the colonial gentry for there were some families of importance which never attained to the dignity of that office. Yet in most colonies the prominent families that never placed a single member on the governor's council were very few indeed, and the councilors at any given date almost always constituted a representative sample of the local aristocracy. A list of all the men who served on the various colonial councils for the hundred years before the Revolution would certainly include 90 per cent of the names of the great "first families" of colonial America.

In all the colonies, and especially in those under royal control, the council was one of the most significant agencies of govern-

[1] William S. Perry, ed., *Historical Collections Relating to the American Colonial Church* ([Hartford, Conn.], 1870–78), III, 126; Cecil Headlam, ed., *Calendar of State Papers, Colonial Series, America and West Indies, 1722–1723* (London: His Majesty's Stationery Office, 1934), p. 330.

ment. It served in a threefold capacity: as the upper house of the
legislature, as the supreme court of the province, and as the
governor's advisory body in executive matters.[2] Upon the death
or absence of the governor and lieutenant governor, the senior
councilor became acting governor.[3] Thus by constitutional
right the council had a definite share in each of the three great
branches of government. The council did not succeed in every
colony in exercising all the power its position nominally gave
it. Sometimes it found itself ground between the upper and
lower millstones of a royal governor and a popular assembly or
became merely an auxiliary of one or the other of these powerful contestants in their perennial battles. But even if its technical
position was sometimes weak, its political weight was usually
considerable, both because its members so often exercised an
important if indirect control in the election of assemblymen, as
has been pointed out, and because it was able to influence the
policies of so many of the governors.

The colonial council normally consisted of twelve men. In
the royal colonies members were appointed by the king and in
the proprietary colonies by their proprietors. In both instances
councilors held office during "pleasure," which meant that they
normally served for life. Ordinarily, men were recommended
for vacancies by the royal governors, although more than once
an aspirant was able to obtain appointment in the face of stren-
uous opposition by the governor through the help of influential
friends in England. But even when the governor nominated he
was limited in his choice of candidates. His instructions directed
him to "take care that they be men of good life and well affected
to our government, and of good estates and abilities, and not

[2] The Pennsylvania council is an exception. After 1701 it was only
an executive body, although for a time it also acted as a court of
chancery.

[3] From 1707 on. Before that date the entire council, with the senior
councilor presiding, served as acting governor.

necessitous persons or much in debt."⁴ With the possible exception of the last, these phrases came as close as any could to describing the type of person who constituted the colonial gentry we are considering.

In Virginia, as society was constituted, practically the only men "of good estates and abilities, and not necessitous persons" who could possibly be nominated were the members of the little group of planter aristocrats.⁵ And who was there to deny that above all others they were Virginia's men "of good life"? Thus it came about that a relatively few families of wealth and social distinction provided the largest part of the membership of the council, and since their families were nearly all intermarried, the council became a body of uncles, cousins, and brothers-in-law, who, when they put up a united front, were often able to guide their relatives and supporters in the lower house, checkmate the governor at any hostile move, and run the colony generally in the interests of their own extremely privileged class.

The extent of this group domination can be seen from an analysis of its personnel.⁶ From 1680, when the journals first be-

⁴ Leonard W. Labaree, ed., *Royal Instructions to British Colonial Governors, 1670–1776* (New York: D. Appleton-Century Company, 1935), I, 55–56. In 1728 the words "or much in debt" were dropped. In the case of a colonial, especially of a Southern planter, this was too idealistic a qualification. Some further changes were introduced in the formula in 1756 but without altering the meaning.

⁵ The commissary of the Bishop of London was, however, regularly appointed a member of the council. Here, and in many other colonies the surveyor general of the customs for the district usually held a seat ex officio.

⁶ The following survey of the councils of eleven colonies is based upon a year-by-year check of the council journals, wherever available, supplemented by collected lists of councilors such as are to be found in William G. and Mary N. Stanard, comps., *The Colonial Virginia Register* (Albany, N.Y.: Joel Munsell's Sons, 1902); William H. Whitmore, *The Massachusetts Civil List for the Colonial and Provincial Periods, 1630–1774* (Albany, N.Y., 1870); the Appendixes of the *Acts of the*

gin to be complete, to the Revolution, ninety-one men received appointment to the Virginia council. Only fifty-seven family names, however, are represented on the list. Of these, nine names account for just short of a third of the total membership.[7] Almost another third came from the next fourteen names.[8] Thus, during a period equal to the time from the Mexican War to the Second World War, over 60 per cent of the places on the council were occupied by members of only twenty-three families. But these figures only begin to suggest the solidarity of the council for they fail to show the extensive intermarriage within the group. That situation can well be illustrated by reference to the descendants of Lucy Higginson, a Virginia lady who lived in the middle of the seventeenth century. By two of her three husbands, Lewis Burwell and Philip Ludwell, themselves early councilors, she was the direct ancestor of seven councilors and of the wives of eight others.[9] One sixth of all Virginia councilors

---

Privy Council of England, Colonial Series (Hereford and London: His Majesty's Stationery Office, 1908–12); etc. The data on family relationships have been gathered from too widely scattered sources to be listed here. Most useful, however, have been articles on the genealogies of many important families in local historical journals, such as *Virginia Magazine of History and Biography, South Carolina Historical Magazine, Maryland Historical Magazine, Pennsylvania Magazine of History and Biography,* and *New England Historical and Genealogical Register.* In gathering the genealogical information summarized in this chapter I have had the able assistance of Dr. Thomas G. Manning, Mr. George Kleman, and Mr. Treat Clark Hull.

[7] The Page family contributed five members of the council; the Burwell, Byrd, Carter, Custis, Harrison, Lee, Ludwell, and Wormley families, three each.

[8] The following were the surnames of two councilors each during the period under consideration: Beverley, Blair, Corbin, Dawson, Digges, Fairfax, Grymes, Lewis, Lightfoot, Nelson, Randolph, Robinson, Smith, and Taloe.

[9] The surnames included are: Bassett, Berkeley, Burwell, Byrd, Grymes, Lee, Ludwell, Nelson, Page, and Parke.

after 1680 could refer to the good lady as "Grandmother Lucy." Many of the men in this group were related to each other twice or three times over, and most were also related to several other councilors. In fact, for any one time during this period a roster of the Virginia council shows from a third to a half of the members were closely related to one or more other councilors and more distantly connected by blood or marriage with various others.

These family relationships were a source of power to the Virginia councilors throughout the period. They did not always agree among themselves, and there were the same number of personal dislikes and jealousies as in most large family groups. But they could and did unite on matters in which their mutual interests were at stake, sometimes at the expense of the wider interest of the colony as a whole. The royal governors often found the family solidarity of the council membership an obstacle to their plans quite as serious as the opposition of the House of Burgesses. Two able, though strong-minded and pugnacious governors, Sir Edmund Andros and Francis Nicholson, were driven from office chiefly by conciliar opposition. Governor Alexander Spotswood's difficulties were more protracted. He undertook various badly needed reforms in the affairs of the colony which antagonized not only the debtor class but also the great officeholding planters who dominated the council.[10] Spotswood's archenemies on the council were William Byrd II, receiver-general; Philip Ludwell, deputy auditor, who was an uncle of Byrd's wife; and the Reverend James Blair, commissary of the Bishop of London, and Ludwell's brother-in-law. The

[10] Documents on this controversy were gathered and reprinted by Worthington C. Ford in *The Controversy between Lieutenant-Governor Spotswood, and His Council and the House of Burgesses, on the Appointment of Judges on Commissions of Oyer and Terminer. 1718* (Winnowings in American History. Virginia Tracts, II. Brooklyn: Historical Printing Club, 1891).

governor enlivened many a letter to England with his diatribes against the family domination of the council and the other leading offices of government. In 1716 he wrote that he would like to suspend Ludwell from the council for obstruction and malfeasance in office. But his hands were tied, he said, for his instructions required the consent of a majority of the council for a suspension, and the Ludwell-Burwell clan held eight of the twelve seats on the board.[11] A year later an action that Spotswood brought against Ludwell in the name of the king could not come to trial in the General Court for lack of a quorum because half of the attending councilors who composed that body were Ludwell's relatives and so were disqualified from sitting on the case.[12] Again and again the governor was frustrated by what he called a "hereditary faction of designing men," a group characterized by "the haughtiness of a Carter, the hypocrisy of a Blair, the inveteracy of a Ludwell, the brutishness of a Smith, the malice of a Byrd, the conceitedness of a Grymes, and the scurrility of a Corbin, with about a score of base disloyalists and ungrateful Creolians for their adherents."[13] Later on, Spotswood decided to become a great Virginia landholder himself, so he composed his differences with these local aristocrats. Then by a process of friendly logrolling in the council, which controlled the distribution of land, he made himself a series of grants, mostly through dummies, and left the governorship the

[11] R. A. Brock, ed., *The Official Letters of Alexander Spotswood, Lieutenant-Governor of the Colony of Virginia, 1710–1722* (Collections of the Virginia Historical Society, New Series, I and II, Richmond, 1882, 1885), II, 151–58; *Cal. State Paps., Col., 1716–17*, No. 171.

[12] *Spotswood Letters*, II, 230; *Cal. State Paps., Col., 1716–17*, No. 522.

[13] *Cal. State Paps., Col., 1717–18*, No. 799. The men referred to in addition to Blair, Ludwell, and Byrd were: Robert ("King") Carter, councilor and agent of the proprietor of the Northern Neck; John Smith, councilor; John Grymes, deputy auditor, a leading burgess, son-in-law of Ludwell, and later a councilor; and Gawin Corbin, a leading burgess and brother-in-law of Edmund Jennings, the senior councilor.

owner of some eighty-five thousand acres of good Virginia land.[14]

Family dominance continued to be a feature of the Virginia council throughout the eighteenth century, although Spotswood's immediate successor, Hugh Drysdale, seems to have been more reconciled to the situation than some of his predecessors. When recommending John Carter, secretary of the colony, to fill a vacancy in 1732, Drysdale warned the Board of Trade that they might object to this appointment since the secretary's father, "King" Carter, was already on the council. He did not add, as he might have done, that a brother-in-law of the candidate, Mann Page, was also a councilor. The lieutenant governor did point out to the home officials, however, that the interrelationship of councilors was inevitable since "there is scarce a qualified person in the colony, unattended with some like inconvenience, for they are all incorporated either in blood or marriages." If the Board of Trade should think the relationship of father and son in the case of the Carters was too close, wrote Drysdale, he could offer them a Hobson's choice in the person of Philip Grymes, the receiver-general, who was merely the son-in-law of a different councilor, Philip Ludwell.[15] The Board of Trade solved the problem neatly by choosing one of the two candidates for the current vacancy and giving the next appointment to the other. The condition of affairs that this incident typified continued unchanged down to the Revolution. When the war began, ten of the twelve members of the council were related to one or more of their colleagues and all but two were sons or grandsons of former councilors.[16]

[14] For an account of Spotswood's administration, see Leonidas Dodson, *Alexander Spotswood, Governor of Colonial Virginia, 1710–1722* (Philadelphia: University of Pennsylvania Press, 1932).

[15] Public Record Office, Colonial Office 5:1319, pp. 298–99; *Cal. State Paps., Col., 1722–23*, No. 738.

[16] One of the two exceptions on each count was the Reverend John

In the other Southern Colonies a situation very much like that in Virginia prevailed, though it was not quite as pronounced.[17] The later date of settlement in the Carolinas naturally reduced slightly the number of intermarriages which had taken place among leading families before the Revolution, but in South Carolina the concentration of social and political life in Charles Town tended to offset this circumstance. William Bull, for example, was one of the first royal councilors; he was the father of another councilor and the grandfather of a third. Three of his daughters married into the Drayton and Middleton families, which provided seven councilors during the royal period. These families, in turn, were connected with the Izards and they with the Blakes, Fenwickes, and Pinckneys, all of which families were represented on the royal council. These seven interrelated families accounted for a quarter of all the councilors of South Carolina during the royal period. Throughout these years the great majority of the councilors were wealthy planters or city merchants, with a considerable addition of royal officials toward the end of the period. Both types tended to support the administration and to take a conservative view of all important issues.[18]

There was considerably less interrelation within the North Carolina council than in most of the other Southern Colonies, partly because of the diverse character of its settlements. The Albemarle section never achieved as highly developed an aristocracy as did other parts, and the inhabitants of that area had relatively little to do with those who lived in other sections of

Camm, a virtual ex-officio appointee, since he was the commissary of the Bishop of London.

[17] I have omitted Georgia from this study since its settlement and the establishment of its royal government came too late to permit the development of a social and political system on a par with those of the other colonies long before the Revolution.

[18] See W. Roy Smith, *South Carolina as a Royal Province, 1719–1776* (New York: The Macmillan Company, 1903), p. 87.

the colony. Further south, and especially in the Cape Fear region, however, there were more men of wealth and position whose families intermarried and who tended to monopolize the best public offices and dominate the council. Among such families, the McCulloughs, the Drys, and the Moores were conspicuous. Close personal and business ties bound groups of families together as in the case of the Innes', Murrays, Corbins, and Rutherfurds, whose heads were members of the council in the fifties. Thus there developed in North Carolina a conciliar aristocracy which differed only in degree, and not in kind, from the groups in the two adjacent colonies.[19]

The Maryland council furnishes a pattern very similar to that of Virginia, though it was complicated by the fact that the colony was a private proprietorship during most of the period. Royal government was instituted in 1691, but in 1715 Maryland was turned back to Lord Baltimore and from that time until the Revolution was administered by the Calvert family. In addition, therefore, to the usual number of large planter families, a special group appeared that was allied by blood, marriage, or political interest to the Calverts and inevitably contributed many members to the provincial council. During the period from 1691 to 1771, seventy-two men received appointment to the royal or proprietary council of Maryland.[20] They represented fifty-five family names. During the first half of the period the council was made up almost exclusively of great landowners, the embodiment of the planter aristocracy, indistinguishable from the men who occupied a similar position in Virginia, ex-

[19] For accounts of some of these relationships and for an entertaining picture of life in the Rutherfurd family on the eve of the Revolution, see Evangeline W. and Charles M. Andrews, eds., *Journal of a Lady of Quality* (3d ed.; New Haven: Yale University Press, 1939).

[20] I have not been able to make my analysis complete for the last years before the Revolution because of the absence of Maryland council journals after 1771.

cept that the Maryland councilors as a group were perhaps inferior in general ability to their Virginia counterparts and that many of them were closely identified in interest with the proprietary system.[21] Toward the middle of the eighteenth century Lord Baltimore began to strengthen his council by the addition of men of marked ability, such as Daniel Dulany the younger (appointed in 1757), who had risen to prominence through the assembly. But certain great families were consistently represented on the council throughout the century. A Tasker was appointed in 1699, his son in 1722, and his grandson in 1745; the first of three Bordleys in 1721, a second in 1759, and a third in 1768. The first Edward Lloyd, himself a mid-seventeenth-century councilor, was the grandfather of three councilors of the eighteenth century, the great-grandfather of a fourth, and the ancestor of the wives of three others. In Governor Sharpe's council of 1753, eight out of eleven members were sons, sons-in-law, or grandsons of former councilors; and there were a father, a father-in-law, and two brothers-in-law of future councilors.[22]

In all the Southern Colonies most of the councilors were owners of great plantations, closely identified with each other in interest and very often in family. As members of the upper

[21] "Almost always, after the restoration of the proprietary government in 1715, the secretary, the commissary general, the attorney general, the agent, the judge or judges of the land office, one or both of the treasurers, the commissioners of the currency office, and the five naval officers were members of the council." Newton D. Mereness, *Maryland as a Proprietary Province* (New York: The Macmillan Company, 1901), p. 177. This is, of course, another way of saying that the choice jobs in the colony were all held by the great landowning members of the council.

[22] Thomas Addison, councilor from 1708 to 1727, appears to have had the most extensive relationship with other councilors of any in Maryland. He was the son of a councilor, son-in-law of another, father-in-law of two, brother-in-law of two, uncle of one, and grandfather of one.

house of the assembly they opposed legislation favored by the small planters at the expense of the great estates, and in general they occupied all the really worth-while offices of government.

Under the Charter of Privileges of 1701 the council in Pennsylvania was less important institutionally than in any of the other proprietary or royal provinces. It had few judicial functions and never sat as a full-fledged upper house of the legislature, but its political influence, especially in the early years of the century, was considerable. It advised the proprietor or his deputy governor on all important matters, including the approval or disapproval of measures sent up by the assembly, and in many other ways acted as a controlling force in the management of affairs.

The assembly, with a distribution of seats which strongly favored the eastern counties, came to be dominated by the rich Quaker merchants of Philadelphia and their political allies. The councilors, on the other hand, appointed by the proprietor and serving during his pleasure, were, next to the governor, the most important bulwark of proprietary interest and authority. They consisted chiefly of proprietary officeholders, large landowners, and friends and relatives of the Penn family.[23] Intermarriage among conciliar families was on the whole not as strikingly frequent in Pennsylvania as in some of the Southern Colonies. Their connection with each other was to a considerable extent through their mutual relationship, personal or political, with the proprietor and his family. Three members of the immediate family served on the council at one time or another, as did several members of the Allen, Asseton, and Hamilton families, allied to the Penns by blood or marriage. The assembly of Penn-

[23] Much useful information on Pennsylvania councilors and their family relationships is to be found in Charles P. Keith, *The Provincial Councillors of Pennsylvania Who Held Office between 1733 and 1776, and those Earlier Councillors Who were Some Time Chief Magistrates of the Province and their Descendants* (Philadelphia, 1883).

sylvania was not noteworthy among provincial legislatures for its liberalism; yet when it advanced measures favored by the colonists but adversely affecting the personal or financial position of the Penns, the assembly found in the council an even more conservative body and as stanch a supporter of vested interests as any of the colonies could produce.

When the Duke of York granted New Jersey to his friends Berkeley and Carteret in 1664, he laid the foundation for what became the most complicated structure of proprietary ownership in all of British North America. Although governmental powers were surrendered to the Crown in 1702, rights to the soil remained in the hands of the proprietors, who consisted at this time of two large groups of both residents and nonresidents, one controlling East Jersey and the other West Jersey. In 1713 Governor Robert Hunter succeeded in breaking the power of a political ring that had been running the colony, and he deliberately inaugurated a policy of cultivating the proprietary interest. To the vacancies on his council he appointed in that year five men who were themselves leading proprietors. Other governors followed the same policy, and with one short interval in the thirties, the council of New Jersey continued subservient to the proprietary interest. The great majority of subsequent appointees to the council were proprietors of either East or West Jersey, and most were among the active leaders of the organized groups of proprietors.[24] With the support of the governors they effectively controlled the executive branch of government for forty years or more. The stranglehold which the landed interests were thus able to maintain over the province had an inevitable sequel: remonstrance by less privileged inhabitants; organized resistance to the proprietors' claims in some

[24] For a discussion of the personnel of the New Jersey council to 1738, see Edwin P. Tanner, *The Province of New Jersey, 1664–1738* ([New York: Columbia University], 1908), chap. xv.

areas, especially in Elizabethtown and other parts of East Jersey; tacit support of the rioters by the assembly; and a temporary breakdown of law and order — all-too-familiar features of conflict between the masses on the one hand and entrenched privilege on the other.

New York, in contrast to Maryland, Pennsylvania, and New Jersey, had no private proprietors in the technical sense after the Duke of York became James II, but it did have a great landed aristocracy. From early times until well after the beginning of the eighteenth century English governors made a practice of granting huge tracts of land to their favorites. Although some of the grants remained unoccupied for long periods of time, others were organized into manors or great estates with numerous tenant farmers and were administered for the benefit of the landlords. In addition to the largest tracts, the governors made many other grants only less princely in extent, in direct or indirect violation of royal instructions limiting the size of their land grants. As a result there grew up in New York a class of great landowners, who were soon recognized as the aristocrats of the province. They, with their allies, the merchants and later the lawyers, came to dominate the politics of the colony. Much as in Virginia, the heads of the great families occupied seats on the governor's council and through controlled elections placed their relatives and dependents in the assembly.[25]

In his study of the party system in New York on the eve of

[25] An excellent discussion of the whole subject of agrarian control of New York politics, which supplements the material I had already gathered before its publication, and upon which I have heavily relied in this section, is in Irving Mark, *Agrarian Conflicts in Colonial New York, 1711–1715* (New York: Columbia University Press, 1940), especially chap. iii. See also C. W. Spencer, "Sectional Aspects of New York Provincial Politics," *Political Science Quarterly*, XXX (September 1915), 397–424; and Carl L. Becker, *The History of Political Parties in the Province of New York, 1760–1776* (Bulletin 286 of the University of Wisconsin, "History Series," II, No. 1. Madison, 1909).

the Revolution, Carl Becker has listed the seventeen families with the largest active estates in the province. Thirteen of these had representatives on the council, constituting a quarter of its total membership during the whole period.[26] As another writer, Irving Mark, has pointed out, "of the twenty-eight councillors who sat at some time between 1750 [and] 1776, at least twenty-five bore the names of conspicuously large landowning families."[27] The figures for the period before 1750 are almost as striking.

This monopoly of the New York council by the landed aristocracy is even more marked if intermarriage within the leading families is considered. Nowhere, even in Virginia, was there a more extensive system of family alliances. So numerous and so varied were the ties between groups that it is seldom safe to say without prolonged investigation that any two leading families were definitely unconnected. The classic illustration of this interrelationship, often cited, is the list of those who attended the funeral of Abraham DePeyster in 1767. More than one hundred relatives were present, bearing twenty-five different family names.[28] Of these names, fifteen were represented at one time or another on the New York council, six at the very time of the funeral.

[26] Becker, *Political Parties*, pp. 8–9. The seventeen great families were: Bayard, De Lancey, DePeyster, Heathcote, Johnson, Livingston, Morris, Nicoll, Pell, Philipse, Rapalje, Remsen, Schuyler, Smith, Stuyvesant, Van Cortlandt, and Van Rensselaer. He includes Fordham Manor among the important estates but it passed out of the hands of a single family relatively early. Between 1691 and 1775 all these family names appeared on the council roll except Pell, Rapalje, Remsen, and Stuyvesant.

[27] Mark, *Agrarian Conflicts*, p. 92. Among important names mentioned by Mark in this connection but omitted from Becker's more limited list are: Alexander, Clarke, Colden, Horsmanden, Kennedy, Reade, and Watts.

[28] Becker, *Political Parties*, p. 13; Mark, *Agrarian Conflicts*, pp. 87–88; Alexander C. Flick, ed., *History of the State of New York* (New York: Columbia University Press, 1933–37), III, 148–51.

This interrelationship of the New York aristocracy did not mean that its leaders always worked together in harmony. On the contrary, Cadwallader Colden and James De Lancey, for example, hated and fought each other for years, even though Colden's daughter was De Lancey's sister-in-law.[29] But it did mean, in the first place, that the landed aristocracy as a class controlled the politics of the province to the almost complete exclusion of less privileged classes, and, in the second place, that when matters of mutual concern were at stake the great families could, and usually did, unite to defend their interests and the interests of their class. In 1699 Governor Bellomont's bill to annul several large land grants was opposed in council by Stephen Van Cortlandt, Robert Livingston, and William Smith, who themselves owned, respectively, 86,000 acres in Westchester, 160,000 acres in Dutchess County, and 50 square miles on Long Island. During and after the antirent agitation of 1766 and 1767 William Smith II and William Alexander sat as judges on cases materially affecting their relative, Robert Livingston, Jr.; one can be sure that the landed interest did not lose by their decisions.[30] All in all, there were no colonies north of the Mason and Dixon Line and few south of it so dominated in their political organization

[29] In 1749 Colden charged his rival with nepotism in using his influence to secure the appointment of his relatives and dependents to council vacancies in order to control that body. Later Colden was himself guilty of attempting the same thing at the expense of the De Lancey faction. *Letters and Papers of Cadwallader Colden . . . . 1711–1775* (Collections of the New-York Historical Society, New York, 1918–23, 1934–35), IX, 20–21; *The Colden Letter Books* (Collections of the New-York Historical Society, 1876, 1877), I, 5–6; Edmund B. O'Callaghan, ed., *Documents Relative to the Colonial History of the State of New York* (Albany, N.Y., 1853–87), VII, 444, 445. (The last-named collection is hereafter cited as *N. Y. Col. Docs.*)

[30] These incidents and others of a like nature are mentioned by Mark, *Agrarian Conflicts*, pp. 90–91. See also *N. Y. Col. Docs.*, IV, 510; *Colden Letter Books*, I, 231; II, 70.

and life by a small but privileged class as New York was by its great families.

The story of the New Hampshire council, especially in the later years, is the story of the aggrandizement of a single family, the Wentworths. The colonial period offers no example to match the overwhelming control over a province's higher offices that the Wentworth family won in New Hampshire. Their record is worth describing in some detail.

John Wentworth, the first of the family to attain important office, became lieutenant governor of the province in 1717. At that time the fathers-in-law of two of his children were already on the council as well as another gentleman who was destined a few years later to become his son-in-law. During the years of his lieutenant governorship another son-in-law, a brother-in-law, and the grandfather of his son's wife became councilors.

In 1741 John Wentworth's eldest son, Benning, who had served briefly as a councilor in the period after his father's death, became the first separate governor of New Hampshire. At the start his council included the governor's three brothers-in-law, an uncle by marriage, and two other men somewhat more remotely connected with him. During the twenty-five long years of Wentworth's service, he managed to secure the addition to his council of a brother and two nephews. In 1766 John Wentworth the younger succeeded his uncle as governor and served until the Revolution. His instructions renewed the appointment to the council of the new governor's father, a first cousin, and an uncle by marriage, and added for the first time an uncle, another uncle by marriage, a first cousin once removed, a step-cousin, and the husband of a cousin. As John Wentworth had been in England when named to office, it is not likely that chance alone thus brought eight of the twelve council seats into the possession of the new governor's relatives. Nor was he idle during the years that followed. Before the outbreak of the Revolution an uncle by marriage, a cousin by marriage, and a first cousin once removed had found welcome places at the council board.[31]

On the whole, the Wentworths did rather well by themselves. Of the men who actually sat on the New Hampshire council during the governorships of Benning and John Wentworth, exactly one half were connected by blood or marriage with the family.[32] Eleven of the sixteen councilors who served at one time or another under the younger John Wentworth were his relatives. When it is remembered that most of the high judicial and administrative offices were filled, in New Hampshire as elsewhere, by councilors; that the governor and his council together were empowered to grant land; that the Wentworth administrations coincided with the period of the "New Hampshire grants" west of the Connecticut River, in conflict with New York's claims to the same territory; and that the Wentworths, especially Benning, profited enormously from the consequent land jobbery — when all of these factors are considered, one can only marvel that the Privy Council allowed this family to continue its monopoly of the government.

In the New England colonies of Massachusetts, Connecticut, and Rhode Island, the councilors, or assistants as they were called in the latter two, were on a somewhat different footing from elsewhere. Instead of being appointed by king or proprietor and serving during pleasure, they were annually elected, in Massachusetts according to the Charter of 1691 by the legislature, in Connecticut and Rhode Island by the freemen of the colony. Furthermore, the less sharply defined social stratification of these colonies, together with the system of town organi-

[31] In 1773 nine of the twelve councilors were the governor's relatives by blood or marriage; including his father and father-in-law.

[32] In compiling these figures I have omitted from the reckoning three relatives of the Wentworth family who never assumed the council seats to which they were appointed.

zation, which resulted in a wider distribution of organized community life, produced less intermarriage among members of the upper circle than was common in the other provinces. Nevertheless, an examination of the annual election returns reveals some significant information about those at the top of the political hierarchy in New England.

The Connecticut Charter of 1662 provided that the freemen of the colony should elect annually a governor, a deputy governor, and twelve assistants. Much as in the royal colonies, the assistants participated in the legislative, executive, and judicial activities of the colony. A curious system of choice prevailed. According to this method the freemen nominated twenty men each autumn to stand for election. From this list the same freemen voted for the governor, deputy governor, and twelve assistants in the following May. Almost invariably the incumbent officeholders were renominated and normally they were reelected. As individuals died or retired — or sometimes were defeated — those below in the standing moved up, and new names were added at the bottom of the list. With life and health, a man might hope to advance in time from twentieth nominee to twelfth assistant. From that point he might look forward to moving steadily up the ladder toward the top of the list of assistants. The deputy governorship, when vacated, might be filled by promoting the senior assistant, but more commonly a somewhat younger man a little farther down the list was advanced. The move from the deputy governorship to the governorship might involve a considerable wait, but if the deputy governor succeeded in outliving his superior he was reasonably sure to make the final step to the top. Thus in the Connecticut system the principle of seniority played an important part.

The result, as one might expect, was a magistracy of experience and long service. Analysis of the annual lists shows that among the 111 men who served as assistants, deputy governors,

and governors between the first election under the Charter of
1662 and the Declaration of Independence, the average individual was elected and re-elected fourteen times.[33] The longest
record was held by Roger Walcott, chosen assistant twenty-six
times, deputy governor nine times, and governor three times.
With one two-year break early in his career, he served a total
of thirty-eight years as a magistrate of the colony. Two men,
John Hamlin and William Pitkin, were each elected for thirty-
six consecutive years, the former, unfortunately, putting in
seventeen years as the senior assistant without ever attaining the
deputy governorship. Such cases were a little extreme but not
unduly so. Thirty per cent of the men on the entire list served
twenty years or more.

Such a practice of electing the same men to office again and
again, as prevailed in Connecticut, is usually an indication of a
conservative attitude on the part of both the electorate and the
officials chosen. To elect new men to office when the old are still
candidates normally signifies a desire to change policies or practices of government; to retain the same officeholders year in and
year out means a general contentment with things as they are,
an unwillingness to experiment or disturb the *status quo*, and a
resistance to change. So it often is today in the election of Southern senators and representatives; so it was also in colonial Connecticut. The repeated re-election of the same men to the
magistracy was an indication that the freemen of the colony

---

[33] The median is 11. The 14-year average length of service in Connecticut compares with an average for the Virginia council of 12.6 years.
The Connecticut assistants, though annually elected, thus served longer
on the average than the Virginia councilors, who held office "during the
king's pleasure" without limitation of term and were commonly regarded as being on life appointment. Lists of the Connecticut magistrates and nominees have been compiled from J. Hammond Trumbull
and Charles J. Hoadly, eds., *The Public Records of the Colony of Connecticut* (Hartford, 1850–90).

were satisfied with their political state and the social and religious system it reflected. Both the voting freemen and their elected representatives were stanch supporters of the "standing order."

As already intimated, it is not possible to find as close a family relationship among Connecticut councilors as in some of the other colonies already considered. But some family names do recur with extraordinary consistency. At least one member of the Walcott family was elected in sixty-nine of the one hundred and fourteen years between the coming of the charter and the Declaration of Independence. The Huntingtons figured successfully in all but four elections from 1747 on. And between 1690 and the Revolution only six years passed without at least one Pitkin among the magistrates. In fact, the ten family names that recur most often account for 40 per cent of all the individual choices made during the entire period.[34] The holders of twenty-five surnames occupied two thirds of all the places in the Connecticut magistracy. These figures coincide almost exactly with those for Virginia.

There was a limited amount of intermarriage among these ruling families, but more important than ties of blood was the identity of interest and attitude. Differences and disagreements took place — the Winthrops quarreled with the Masons, a Walcott was displaced as governor by a Fitch and he by a Pitkin — but most such contests were purely personal or involved temporary issues only. Basically, the members of the dominant group thought alike on all important questions regarding the

---

[34] These families, with the number of individual elections credited to each, are as follows: Pitkin, 98; Allyn, 77; Walcott, 69; Stanley, 66; Talcott, 63; Gold, 60; Burr, 56; Hamlin, 52; Huntington, 47; Wadsworth, 44. Other leading families with two or more magistrates each and a total of more than twenty-five years' service between 1662 and 1776 include: Leete, 42; Law, 35; Winthrop, Mason, and Chester, 30 each; Christophers and Sherman, 27 each.

social, religious, and political order. They believed in the system as established by their ancestors, and only men who believed in it could hope to attain high office in the colony.

As the General Court put it in an address to Governor Winthrop in 1699:

It hath been the endeavors of the freemen of this jurisdiction to be annually electing such men for the prime station and betrustment of public affairs which are men of uprightness, who are studious for the cause and interest of religion, for the propagating the designs of their godly ancestors, which endeavors are still aimed at in pursuance of their duty the attainment whereof is our felicity.[35]

The system erected in the first generation of settlement and confirmed by the Charter of 1662 was to them the ideal system and one that required no change. They and their descendants successfully resisted for generation after generation all proposals to alter the basic political and religious structure of the colony. Not until the Charter of 1662 had been in operation for a century and a half did they give way in the face of strong opposition and allow the substitution of a new and more democratic organic law, the Constitution of 1818. These dominant families and their like-minded supporters made Connecticut not only "the Land of Steady Habits" but also probably the most conservative of all the colonies, in spite of its so-called "republican" system of self-government.

The Massachusetts Charter of 1691 provided for appointment of the governor and lieutenant governor by the king as in the normal royal province, but permitted the election of a council of twenty-eight members by annual vote of the legislature or General Court. In its functions the council was intended to be identical with those in the other royal provinces.

In electing the councilors Massachusetts showed results not

[35] *Winthrop Papers*, Part V (Collections of the Massachusetts Historical Society, 6th Series, III, Boston, 1889), p. 42.

strikingly different from those in Connecticut. There was no clear-cut system of seniority, and there were few terms as long as some in the smaller colony. The average tenure was 10.5 years as compared to Connecticut's 14. But the system of re-electing councilors for consecutive terms was well established.[36] The longest consecutive service was that of Samuel Danforth, who was first elected councilor in 1739 and was still in office in 1774, thirty-six years later, when the elected council was abolished by act of Parliament. His record was closely followed by that of the diarist and judge, Samuel Sewall, who was named councilor in the Charter of 1691 and was thereafter chosen annually for thirty-three successive years.

On occasion the General Court chose as councilors men of comparatively radical tendency, but when this happened the governor had at hand an effective weapon in the form of an absolute veto over the General Court's elections. This defense was particularly effective in excluding from the council those who disagreed with the governor and his conservative supporters in times of conflict or serious crisis. Thus in 1741, when currency inflation had become a burning issue, Governor Belcher vetoed the election of thirteen councilors. Bernard vetoed six men in 1766 and again in 1768, and eleven in 1769, and General Gage rejected thirteen in the final election of 1774.[37] In general, however, the men chosen were sufficiently conservative to satisfy even the most cautious governors. Including these wholesale vetoes by Belcher, Bernard, and Gage, they and the other governors only rejected about 3 per cent of all the choices made throughout the entire period. The remarkable thing is not

[36] The Massachusetts median was 8. Seventeen per cent of the individuals were elected twenty times or more, compared to Connecticut's 30 per cent.

[37] Jerathmeel Bowers, otherwise a relatively inconspicuous figure in the prerevolutionary struggles, had the distinction of being vetoed for the council in nine consecutive years.

the radicalism of a few proposed councilors but the consistent conservatism of the men the General Court chose year in and year out throughout the period. Members of prominent merchant families, such as the Cushings, Hutchinsons, Wheelwrights, and Olivers, were elected more often than any others and gave to the Massachusetts council a character and stability not essentially different from what was to be found in the other royal provinces. Massachusetts, too, had its ruling families who brought a strong element of conservatism to the political leadership of the province.

Rhode Island, the last colony to be considered, is the proverbial exception to the general rule. The Charter of 1663 prescribed the annual election of a governor, deputy governor, and ten assistants, employing phraseology very similar to that of the Connecticut charter. Here, however, no consistent principle developed in the choice of these officials.[38] While a few men monopolized the governorship—Samuel Cranston, for example, was governor for twenty-nine consecutive years—and a few families such as the Greenes, Wantons, Arnolds, Coggeshalls, and Fenners were represented in the magistracy by several members and for substantial periods, the colony never developed a tradition of long consecutive service on the council by the same men. There was no system of advancement toward seniority among the assistants, and the average number of times an individual was chosen was only 5, as compared to Massachusetts' 10.5 and Connecticut's 14. Rhode Island, settled by men whom the other New Englanders considered wayward and radical, seems to have liked frequent change among its magistrates. Perhaps it was already developing the "democratic" doctrine of rotation in office.

[38] Lists of the Rhode Island magistrates have been compiled from John R. Bartlett, ed., *Records of the Colony of Rhode Island and Providence Plantation in New England*, Vols. II–VII (Providence, 1857–62).

That Rhode Island was following a course quite contrary to the generally prevailing theory of what was fitting is apparent from the comments of its neighbors. For example, the Earl of Bellomont, governor of New York and Massachusetts, conducted an investigation into the affairs of Rhode Island in 1699 and reported that "the assistants or councillors, who are also justices of the peace and judges of their courts, are generally Quakers, and sectaries, elected by the prevailing factions among them; illiterate and of little or no capacity, several of them not able to write their names, or at least so as to be read, unqualified to exercise their respective offices. . . . whilst several gentlemen most sufficient for estate, best capacitated and disposed for His Majesty's service, are neglected and no ways employed in any office or place in the government, but on the contrary maligned for their good affection to His Majesty's service."[39] When on the very eve of the Revolution Governor Thomas Hutchinson of Massachusetts held his famous interview with George III, the King remarked that Rhode Island was "a strange form of government." The conservative descendant of Anne Hutchinson, the Antinomian rebel, sadly agreed. "They approach, Sir," he said, "the nearest to a democracy of any of your colonies. Once a year all power returns to the people and all their officers are new elected. By this means the governor has no judgment of his own, and must comply with every popular prejudice."[40]

The political equalitarianism of Rhode Island serves to emphasize the aristocratic and conservative tendencies of all the other colonies. The councils in the royal and proprietary provinces represented, for the most part, a closely knit group of ruling families. In those colonies where the councilors or assistants were elected special privilege and economic class were not

[39] *Rhode Island Col. Recs.*, III, 387.
[40] Peter Orlando Hutchinson, comp., *The Diary and Letters of His Excellency Thomas Hutchinson, Esq.* (Boston, 1884), I, 172.

quite so apparent, but even in Massachusetts and Connecticut the repeated choice of the same men and their descendants demonstrates the presence there of well-stabilized ruling groups. Everywhere but in Rhode Island, whether councilors were appointed by king or proprietor, or elected by the enfranchised voters or their representatives, it was assumed, tacitly or openly, that only those who represented "the better sort" were entitled to sit in the upper house of the legislature, to act as judges in the highest court of the colony, and to advise the governor on affairs of state. And by "the better sort" it was clear that people meant not the ablest brains, not even necessarily the shrewdest politicians, but rather those who by inheritance or acquisition owned the largest estates, had the best family connections, and most firmly supported the existing political system, be that system royal or proprietary province or self-governing Puritan colony.

Firm support of the existing order was a leading criterion in Massachusetts and Connecticut. There the legal establishment of the Puritan Church and the backing still given to that Church by the large majority of the voting inhabitants in the eighteenth century — even though other sects might enjoy some toleration — maintained in these colonies an especially close relation between Church and State. Men who objected to the system were not likely to be chosen to high office, regardless of their other qualifications; those who were so constantly elected and re-elected were, with few exceptions, dedicated to the continuance of that system, to the maintenance of its religious and social basis, and to the preservation of the political and economic independence upon which it so largely rested. The dominant political groups in these colonies, typified by the assistants or councilors, might seem to the British to be upholding radical or even republican views, yet, quite as much as the aristocrats of the Virginia or Pennsylvania councils, they represented a privileged interest and defended an existing system against change from within or from without.

The consistent choice as councilors in such colonies as Maryland, Pennsylvania, and New Jersey of those who supported the proprietary interest is a reminder that there still were in America, even as late as the Revolution, vestiges of a system which traced back in origin to feudal times. Although little was left by the mid-eighteenth century of strictly feudal concepts in the organization of these provinces, there yet remained one important principle from an earlier age. All ungranted land in these colonies belonged, not to the public, nor even to the king as the embodiment of the state, but to a single proprietor or a limited group of proprietors, who might deal with it — holding it or disposing of it on terms — to his or their own best advantage without consulting the wishes of the community at large. For the successful exploitation of this principle and for the protection of proprietary interests, whether in the efficient collection of quit-rents or in the exemption of proprietary estates from taxation, the lords of the land needed the support of government. In all three colonies the council provided that support. Composed in Maryland and Pennsylvania chiefly of officeholders, great landowners, and other beneficiaries of the proprietary regime, and in New Jersey of men who were themselves proprietors, the councils of all three colonies were bulwarks of the system, strongholds of privilege. In supporting the proprietorships the councils of these colonies were upholding the greatest single vested interest in colonial America.

In other provinces, such as Virginia and New York where the title to the ungranted land remained in the king, the councils represented a somewhat different principle. In these colonies, fortunes, social standing, and general prestige were to a large extent measured by the number of a man's acres. The great landowners were the "tycoons" of the day. By their membership on the colonial councils, and to some extent by their indirect control of the assemblies, the great families were able to exploit their position for the benefit of their own class. When land was being granted, they were in the council to do the granting along with the governor and to see that a substantial share came to their friends and to themselves. When necessary measures were put forth to control the marketing of the crop or to apportion taxes, they were in a position to divert the full weight of the burden from their own shoulders to those of less privileged groups. When judicial controversy arose over matters affecting the interests of their class, they and their relatives sat on the highest courts and saw that the "right" judgments were handed down. In these royal provinces the system was not designed to safeguard the special interests of a single proprietor, as it was in Maryland and Pennsylvania, but it was, nonetheless, an expression of an aristocratic principle. A relatively small group of men, the "men of good life" and "of good estates and abilities," the "principal gentlemen," or the "gentlemen of weight in the country," as two royal governors described them, occupied the seats on the councils as well as the chief administrative posts and lucrative offices and, from that coign of vantage, manipulated affairs of state in the interests of their own aristocratic class.

The close family connections that existed between the councilors in so many of the provinces is evidence of the class solidarity of the privileged group in eighteenth-century America. Although Virginia, New York, and New Hampshire afford the best examples of this situation, the tendency was present to a greater or lesser degree almost everywhere. The provincial aristocracy was composed of a relatively small group, and in every colony the members of that group were firmly bound together by ties of kinship as well as of social and economic interest. Although they might quarrel among themselves, the colonial gentry could and usually did offer a united front to the outside world, whether that world was represented at the moment by a royal governor or by the great mass of the less privileged populace. Great issues might sometimes divide the aristocracy — as the Revolution itself ultimately did—but in the long course of the years the ruling families maintained a common attitude of conservatism and approval of the *status quo*. In spite of local differences the aristocratic position typified by the provincial councilors was basically the same throughout the colonies, whether it was that of the great landowners of Virginia or New York, the rich merchants of Boston or Charles Town, or the Puritan magistrates of Connecticut. In varying degree and with varying emphasis, the ruling families everywhere upheld the religious, social, and political, as well as the economic, views of the conservative governing class of colonial America.

2

PLANTATION AND COUNTINGHOUSE

One of the important characteristics of the eighteenth-century plantation colonies was the marked distinction between classes, largely based upon differences in the sizes of men's landed estates. In all the colonies individual holdings varied in extent, but in the North generally, and especially in New England and New Jersey, very large acreages were few in number and the contrast between the greatest and the smallest was relatively slight. Except among the great landowners of New York and the proprietary favorites of Pennsylvania, an estate of five thousand acres was a rarity. In the South the situation was very different. In Virginia below the Rappahannock River, as early as 1704, before some of the largest holdings were acquired, there were twenty-five individuals who owned at least five thousand acres each. A few estates were from three to five times that size, although the average planter of that time owned probably about five hundred acres.[1] As time went on, the average size of plantations grew, but the estates of the great landowners increased much more than proportionately. By 1750, when the average

[1] The quit-rent roll of 1704 is printed in Thomas J. Wertenbaker, *The Planters of Colonial Virginia* (Princeton: Princeton University Press, 1922), Appendix. My estimate of five hundred acres for the average holding is derived from an analysis of this rent-roll modified by the result of a study of early eighteenth-century Virginia wills made by Dr. C. G. G. Moss in "The Virginia Plantation System: A Study of Economic Conditions in That Colony for the Years 1700 to 1750" (an unpublished doctoral dissertation in the Yale University Library).

Virginia estate was about 750 acres, an important group of individuals owned thirty, fifty, seventy-five, or even one hundred thousand acres apiece. Somewhat similar conditions prevailed in Maryland and South Carolina and in the Hudson Valley of New York.[2] The owners of these vast estates were among the great figures who dominated the life of their colonies.

Wherever great landowners existed social cleavages appeared. Thomas Anburey, a British officer in Burgoyne's surrendered army, declared that before the Revolution "the spirit of equality or leveling principle" was less prevalent in Virginia than in the other provinces; in the Old Dominion the different classes of people "supported a greater distinction" than those elsewhere.[3] Other travelers reported the same thing. In general, contemporary observers and later historians have agreed that three distinct classes existed in the plantation colonies. At the top were the great landowners, the men whom Anburey called the "gentlemen of the best families and fortunes."[4] Below them came the small planters and yeomen farmers, the 80 per cent of landowners with estates of less than a thousand acres. The third class included the lowly indentured servants and the Negro slaves.

Of these three classes the first is the subject of our present consideration. The "first gentlemen" who composed it, and their counterparts among the few great landholders of the northern provinces, were the men who dominated the social life

[2] If I seem to lay a disproportionate emphasis, here and in the following pages, on Virginia, it is because material on that colony is so much more abundant than on any of the other plantation colonies. In general, what is said of Virginia is borne out by the available evidence on the other regions that had a great landholding class.

[3] [Thomas Anburey], *Travels through the Interior Parts of America. In a Series of Letters* (London, 1789), II, 370.

[4] *Ibid.*, II, 371. The leading merchants of the Carolinas and Maryland and the few great merchant princes of Virginia, such as Thomas Nelson and Philip Lightfoot, belonged socially and politically in this class.

of these colonies and largely controlled local politics. Being, in general, the beneficiaries of the existing state of affairs they were naturally anxious for it to continue without material change. In their own agricultural communities they were, above all others, the spokesmen of conservative thought and action.

The governor's council was composed almost exclusively of these men. In many instances they also succeeded in controlling the election of a majority of the colonial assembly. To some extent, perhaps, they enjoyed their political leadership simply because they liked "the great game of politics." More often, the prestige that went with high office was the lure that induced them to assume the responsibilities and the frequent long journeys to meetings of council and assembly which were the penalties of public life. There was, too, a tacit assumption that these burdens were the natural duties of men in their station. Like the English country gentlemen, upon whom they modeled so much of their existence, they took it for granted that public service was a part of the life of the gentry, no more to be neglected than decency of dress or generally polite behavior. Beyond all these considerations, however, there is no question but that many of these colonial gentlemen valued their political authority for the very tangible and material rewards it brought. Political activity might be a game, an honor, or a duty, but it was also a very profitable occupation.

It was profitable in a number of ways, most of all because it put these men in a position to increase their landholdings. Land was granted in the royal colonies by the governor and council, and in Maryland by a land office with which the councilors maintained very close connections. Theoretically the home authorities imposed careful restrictions upon the granting of land, but the system as administered left plenty of room for abuse by those on the "inside." The large landowners who composed the council, and their friends and relatives, were very much on the "inside." Even before the beginning of the eighteenth century there were complaints that the Virginia councilors were engrossing the best lands to the disadvantage of poorer men and to the detriment of the colony as a whole. In 1696 Edward Randolph reported that the inhabitants were discouraged "because the members of the council there and others, who make an interest in the government, have from time to time procured grants of very large tracts" so that for many years there had been no waste land to be taken up by newcomers. Late arrivals and released servants were forced to rent land or go to the more dangerous and difficult frontier sections.[5]

The eighteenth century saw an increase rather than a lessening in the land-grabbing activities of the Virginia gentry. The *Council Journals* show that grants to councilors, their relatives, and their associates, were increasing steadily both in number and in size, and scattered references imply clearly that by no means all the grants actually made were entered on the journals. Some individuals or associations of individuals received grants of extraordinary size. Councilor William Bassett and his son-in-law Gawin Corbin received 15,000 acres in 1720, and Corbin got 3,000 more in the same year. Councilor John Carter was granted 20,000 acres in 1728 and 6,000 more in the next year. A group headed by Councilor William Randolph received four separate grants in 1738 totaling no less than 104,000 acres. Even exclud-

---

[5] *Cal. State Paps., Col., 1696–97*, No. 176, cited in Wertenbaker, *Planters of Colonial Virginia*, p. 142, and Louis B. Wright, *The First Gentlemen of Virginia: Intellectual Qualities of the Early Colonial Ruling Class* (San Marino, Calif.: The Huntington Library, 1940), pp. 55–56. The most recent and thorough discussion of land-grabbing in Virginia is in Thomas J. Wertenbaker, *The Old South: The Founding of American Civilization* (New York: Charles Scribner's Sons, 1942), pp. 311–22. See also [Fairfax Harrison], *Virginia Land Grants. A Study of Conveyancing in Relation to Colonial Politics* (Richmond: privately printed by the Old Dominion Press, 1925).

ing such awards to syndicates of speculating planters as the last, the average individual grant by the 1750's had attained the size of 4,250 acres.[6] Land was still the great source of wealth in the plantation colonies and the landed gentry with connections on the council were favorably placed, not only to hold their own, but even to improve their relative economic position.

The large landholdings of these gentlemen in the newly opened regions of the West were of advantage to them in two ways. As the inefficient and wasteful system of agriculture, especially of tobacco culture, led to the rapid exhaustion of the soil, it became imperative for the planter to acquire new land onto which to transfer his Negroes and from which he could raise the crops that would yield a satisfactory income. The small planter of the tidewater counties stood, relatively, in just as great need of fresh acreage as did his wealthy neighbor, but as the system worked he was far less likely to get it than was the gentleman of standing and influence. The gentleman, who was a member of the council or who had friends or relatives in high places, had the inside track. Thus it was that to a considerable degree, as the eighteenth century wore on, the rich became richer and the poor became relatively poorer.

In the second place, the men who received these enormous grants were able to profit directly by the constant flow of immigrants into the new regions. Obviously, many of the individuals and syndicates involved were mere speculators. Those who petitioned for the huge grants of ten to a hundred thousand acres so common in the records of the 1740's and 1750's had no intention of opening up and cultivating all of these great tracts themselves. They aimed instead at peopling their grants with settlers, either as purchasers or as tenants. By pre-empting

[6] Henry R. McIlwaine and Wilmer L. Hall, eds., *Executive Journals of the Council of Colonial Virginia*, Vols. III–V, 1705–1754 (Richmond: Virginia State Library, 1928–45), *passim.*

through legal means and at very little direct money outlay many of the very best lands in the fertile West, the great planters of the older, settled regions were able to cash in on the never-ending demand for land from the swarms of newcomers to the back country. Of course the great men of the East did not succeed in controlling all the new land and much illegal squatting on other men's property took place, but in general the wealthy landowners were able to reap rich speculative rewards from their domination of the machinery of land granting throughout the South.

In the matter of political control, however, matters did not work out so easily. As population increased in the Southern Piedmont and the Great Valley, the political and social position of the aristocrats, so firmly entrenched in the tidewater region, began to be threatened. In spite of their large holdings in the West, the great planters could not dominate politically the new settlements as effectively as they had the old. As great numbers of small farmers moved in—some Scots, some Scotch-Irish, some Germans, and some English—they brought with them or developed here new ideas of political and social relationships based far more nearly on principles of equality. Unlike the tidewater planters, they had no direct or continuous contact with England and they had neither the means nor the inclination to pattern their lives on those of English country gentlemen. Few of them had any expectation of becoming great magnates themselves; they were largely raisers of grain, not of tobacco or rice, and so had no need for the large plantations which the efficient cultivation of those staples required. Some worked their own fields with the help of only a few Negroes; others owned no slaves at all. Few felt any real sense of attachment or loyalty to the established Anglican Church, which the easterners upheld as part of the natural and proper scheme of things. Rude and uncultured though they might be, the western settlers were a class of sturdy yeomen, and they refused to recognize the right of any tide-water aristocracy to dominate their lives and fortunes.[7]

The planters of the eastern sections, however, were unwilling to lose control. They were accustomed to leadership. Each had long been "sovereign on his own plantation," as a French traveler had observed as early as 1687;[8] among them they had always divided the great offices, and they controlled the political life of their colonies against influence from without or from within in the interest of their class and section as a whole. For a long time they were able to forestall any serious challenge to their leadership, partly, at least, by denying to the newer settlements legislative representation in just proportion to their growing population. But inevitably conflicts arose. Some, over such questions as taxation, affected primarily the economic interests of the contending groups. Others, such as the licensing of nonconformist meetinghouses and preachers, touched on the principle of religious liberty. Still others, such as issues of representation, the character of local officeholders, and the administration of justice, were fundamental to all problems of intersectional equality. In some of these quarrels the tidewater planters were able to keep the upper hand throughout the colonial period, as they did in the matter of representation in South Carolina. In others, such as the question of religious toleration in Virginia, a working compromise was found. Occasionally, the conflict reached really dangerous proportions and once it broke out into actual hostilities.

I refer to that episode in North Carolina history known as the War of the Regulation. Fundamentally, this affair, which inter-

[7] For an account of the conflict of cultures in the western regions, see Wertenbaker, *The Old South,* chap. v.

[8] [Durand of Dauphiné], *A Huguenot Exile in Virginia: Or Voyages of a Frenchman Exiled for his Religion with a Description of Virginia & Maryland,* edited by Gilbert Chinard (New York: The Press of the Pioneers, 1934), p. 10.

rupted the peace and quiet of the colony from 1768 to 1771, was a conflict between the yeomen settlers of the western counties and the officeholding and privileged class throughout the province. The tax system was such that its burden fell relatively much more heavily on poor men than on those of property; the tax collectors and other officials were inefficient, corrupt, and rapacious; and the distribution of seats in the assembly gave the eastern districts a disproportionate share of the representation. In spite of repeated protests, the small farmers of Orange, Anson, and neighboring counties, where the agitation centered, were unable to win redress of their very real grievances or even a sympathetic hearing for their complaints. Violence broke out, courts were attacked, and twice Governor Tryon called out the militia.

The extent to which class lines determined men's sympathies in this crisis is suggested by the composition of the military force that responded to the governor's first call for troops. Many of the militia privates hung back, but so many mounted officers appeared that to accommodate them Tryon had to form a special troop of "Gentlemen Volunteer Light Dragoons." The less than thirteen hundred privates and noncommissioned officers who formed the so-called "army" had at their head a grand total of twelve colonels and lieutenant colonels, two major generals, and six lieutenant generals.[9] The planter aristocracy of North Carolina was very literally up in arms.

The second military expedition into the disaffected regions culminated in the Battle of Alamance in May 1771, where the insurgents were completely routed. A few of the leading Regulators were captured and executed, and others were outlawed and forced into exile, but the rank and file submitted to authority and were granted pardons. Law and order were restored.

[9] William L. Saunders, ed., *The Colonial Records of North Carolina*, VII (Raleigh, 1890), 889.

Not until 1776, when the new state constitution incorporated many of the reforms sought by the Regulators, did the landed gentry and officeholding class lose control of the domestic situation. Conservative forces had gained another, though a temporary, victory.

Land was the fundamental source of wealth in provincial America and the produce of the land the principal origin of income. But unless the surplus agricultural produce of the colonies could be exchanged for the manufactured articles and other goods which the inhabitants needed, life in America could hardly rise above the bare subsistence level. Very soon, therefore, men began to turn their attention to trade. Some, like the majority of large-scale tobacco planters of Virginia, conducted their own commercial operations, consigning their crops to British merchants for sale abroad and ordering the shipment in return of such European goods as they and their families needed. But for most colonists, whose crops were too small in value or too diversified in character to permit such direct dealings with foreign correspondents, a colonial middleman was a necessary adjunct to trade in both its import and its export branches. The need for commercial intermediaries gave early rise to the colonial merchant; the steady expansion of the colonies and the constantly growing complexity of trade relations made him an increasingly necessary member of society. In colonial America as a whole the merchant was, next to the landowner, the most important element of economic life.

Unlike the great landholders, merchants were to be found in every colony. They were most numerous, of course, in the larger trading centers from Portsmouth, New Hampshire, to Charles Town, South Carolina, but they set up, too, in smaller places such as Lebanon, Connecticut, where Jonathan Trumbull operated, or Cross Creek, North Carolina, at the head of navigation on the Cape Fear River. Even the rivers of Virginia were not immune to their infiltration. Scottish mercantile houses sent over factors to the tobacco regions, where they settled at strategic points, often in the tiniest of hamlets, and catered to the business of the lesser planters in the neighborhood. Wherever trade was possible, there, sooner or later, merchants or their factors found their way.

Strictly speaking, the colonial merchants cannot be called a single social class for they varied too greatly among themselves in wealth and background, from such an aristocrat as the rich Quaker Thomas Wharton of Philadelphia or the patrician Oliver De Lancey of New York to the obscure Scottish apothecary Murdock McLeon of Cross Creek, North Carolina. But merchants everywhere had much in common. As trade among the Continental colonies and with the West Indies increased, the leading merchants of the different sections began to have more and more contact with each other. A great landowner of New York, such as Stephen Van Rennselaer, might scarcely have heard of his South Carolina counterpart, Sir John Colleton, but such a New York merchant as John Watts was in frequent correspondence with other merchants such as John Ewing of Boston, John Riddell of Virginia, or Joseph Maynard of Barbados.[10] Such men had many mutual interests. Not only did they "talk the same language" and often engage in direct business with each other, but they were concerned over the same problems and affected by the same developments. Did the price of good Madiera wine go down? Importers in Boston and Charles Town might both be interested in the chance to make a favorable purchase. Did a New York merchant have an order to send some horses to Barbados? A New Haven shipper might have a vessel which could take them most expeditiously. Did war with France

[10] Dorothy C. Barck, ed., *Letter Book of John Watts, Merchant and Councillor of New York, January 1, 1762–December 22, 1765* (Collections of the New-York Historical Society, New York, 1928).

send insurance rates up and threaten the safety of the West India trade? The Newport slave trader and the Philadelphia provision merchant awaited news of their ventures with equal anxiety. Or did Parliament add to the list of "enumerated commodities" which might legally be shipped only to Great Britain or another colony? Exporters of lumber from New Hampshire and of deerskins from South Carolina might be equally hurt and equally resent the measure.

Trading interests formed a link between the merchants among the different colonies; within a single area the ties were even closer. In the "commercial" colonies of the North and especially in such great seaports, both north and south, as Boston, Newport, New York, Philadelphia, and Charles Town, the merchants were both rich and numerous enough to form practically a distinct class, playing an important part not only in the economic life of their communities but in the social and political spheres as well. In no colony did they so completely dominate the political machinery as the planter class did in Virginia and elsewhere, though they came close to it in Pennsylvania. Yet in each colony where commercial interests were strong the group of leading merchants had an influence on government quite out of proportion to their actual numbers, and in alliance with one or another group of other voters they were often able to maintain a working control of local politics.

In New York, for example, the merchants often found themselves opposed in the municipal common council by the representatives of the artisan-shopkeeper class, and in the provincial assembly the heavy representation of country districts often led to legislation unfavorable to the commercial interest. But at times the merchants were able to form a coalition with the representatives of Albany and of the manors and pocket boroughs and with some of the great landholding families who were interested in trade as well as land. And during the last fifteen years or so of the colonial period nearly all the provincial councilors were either merchants or members of allied landed families.[11]

In South Carolina the fact that many planters maintained houses in Charles Town where they spent the "season" meant a closer bond between them and the merchants of the city. Socially and culturally the two groups had much in common, there was considerable intermarriage among their children, and their economic interests were often parallel when they did not actually coincide. Political ties were consequently close, and much of the time the merchants and great planters constituted practically a single controlling force in public affairs.

The Scottish merchants of the Chesapeake region had a rather different place in colonial affairs. Philip Fithian observed that all the merchants and shopkeepers in the sphere of his acquaintance were young Scots and was told that this was the case throughout Virginia.[12] Their traditional shrewdness made many of them rich but it did not make them popular. A few became wealthy enough to be received socially by the landed gentry, but as a group they never succeeded in breaking into the charmed circle of the planters either socially or politically. Landon Carter put his finger on one explanation of their unpopularity when he pointed out that the Scots never quite assimilated themselves in the community. Although they made their living in the colony, they kept their home connections, their home point of view, and, as far as possible, their Scottish way of life. As Carter said, they "forgot the constant policy of all nations both ancient and modern that when they were at

[11] See Virginia D. Harrington, *The New York Merchant on the Eve of the Revolution* (New York: Columbia University Press, 1935), especially pp. 38–39.

[12] Hunter D. Farish, ed., *Journal and Letters of Philip Vickers Fithian, 1773–1774: A Plantation Tutor of the Old Dominion* (Williamsburg: Colonial Williamsburg, Inc., 1943), p. 39.

Rome to do as the Romans did."[13] Seemingly these Scots could never quite become Virginians, and the Virginians resented it. Fithian, who came from a colony where Scots did assimilate themselves effectively as farmers and in other occupations, was surprised to discover that in some sections of Virginia "Scotchman" was a fighting word. He once saw two "fist battles" break out and wrote in his journal: "The cause of the battles I have not yet known; I suppose either they are lovers and one has in jest or reality in some way supplanted the other; or has in a merry hour called him a 'lubber,' or a 'thickskull,' or a 'buckskin,' or a 'Scotchman.' . . . . All these and ten thousand more quite as trifling and ridiculous are thought and accepted as just causes of immediate quarrels."[14]

Although these Scots never attained a position in Virginia politics comparable to that which other merchants held in other colonies, they were by no means a negligible factor. With a few exceptions, it is true, their direct importance was small, but some of them did have marked influence in their own neighborhoods and as a group they had valuable connections in Great Britain, where the Board of Trade and Privy Council were usually willing to listen to the complaints of British merchants against undesirable legislation in the colonies.

The rich Quaker merchants of Philadelphia were a major element in the political system of Pennsylvania. They were all-powerful in the city itself and they joined with the conservative Quaker and German farmers of the eastern counties to control the assembly. From the beginning of the eighteenth century, the counties of Philadelphia, Chester, and Bucks each sent eight representatives to the legislature, and the city of Philadelphia sent two. These twenty-six assemblymen would have been a

---

[13] "Diary of Colonel Landon Carter," *William and Mary College Quarterly Historical Magazine*, 1st Series, XIV (April 1906), 246–47.
[14] Farish, *Journal and Letters of Fithian*, p. 240.

powerful force even if the newer sections had been given fair representation. But such justice the easterners were unwilling to grant. On a basis of taxes paid, the eastern counties and the city should have had, by 1760, no more than 58 per cent of the total membership; on a basis of population they should have been cut to 48 per cent; they had in fact no less than 72 per cent. By either system of reckoning, Lancaster County should have had more representatives than any other except Philadelphia; instead it had only four against Bucks' and Chester's eight apiece.[15] The wealthy Quaker merchants of the city were the leaders in the political combination. Although socially very close to the supporters of the proprietor who dominated the council, they maintained a separate political organization and fought the proprietor and his governor with marked success. By 1760 the assembly had become in effect "the supreme power in the colony."[16]

In the city of Philadelphia the municipal government was a "closed corporation," the members of the common council filling vacancies among themselves at their own discretion. The franchise within the city for such elective officials as assembly-men, commissioners, and assessors was set extremely high, and the leading merchants customarily drew up the ticket without consulting those "mechanics" and lesser tradesmen who had attained the vote. This monopoly of nominations drew a strong protest on behalf of a group of tradesmen shortly before the Revolution. The inferior voters, their spokesman said, had "tamely submitted" to the great merchants' usurpation "so long that those gentlemen make no scruples to say that the mechanics

[15] The eastern domination of the Pennsylvania assembly is fully discussed in Charles H. Lincoln, *The Revolutionary Movement in Pennsylvania, 1760–1776* (University of Pennsylvania Publications, "Series in History," No. 1, Philadelphia, [1901]). The above percentages are worked out from a table on p. 47.

[16] *Ibid.*, p. 23.

(though by far the most numerous, especially in this county) have no right to be consulted, that is, in fact [they] have no right to speak or think for themselves." The writer objected strenuously to a system under which men were elected "on account of their *greatness* and *opulency*." [17] In spite of such remonstrances the merchants of Philadelphia maintained a system of political control as oligarchic as any in the eighteenth-century colonies.

Colonial merchants in all the colonies constituted, as a group, a strongly conservative force, opposing especially the "radicalism" of the frontier regions. There were several reasons for their attitude. Many of them were men of substantial means. James Birket, a visitor from the West Indies in 1750, was impressed with the wealth and extravagance of the Boston merchants, "amongst whom you will find very good entertainment, and their houses furnished in an elegant manner. Their dress very genteel and in my opinion both men and women are too expensive in that respect." [18] Such comments might have been repeated in all the chief seaports, for not even the Puritan or Quaker teachings of simplicity and otherworldliness could protect all of the more prosperous burghers and their families from the vices of extravagance and ostentation. Such wealth, as nearly always, inculcated in its possessors a sense of superiority and of precedence and led to a jealous guardianship of privilege. Society as constituted had enabled these men to become rich; any change that might make them less rich, absolutely or relatively, was naturally something to oppose with vigor and determination.

The merchants as a group tended to be a conservative force in colonial society, also, because of their British connections. More than any other group, except possibly the great planters

[17] Quoted in *ibid.*, pp. 80–81 n.
[18] *Some Cursory Remarks Made by James Birket in His Voyage to North America, 1750–1751* (New Haven: Yale University Press, 1916), p. 21.

of the South, they were in constant contact with the mother country. More than any other group they could understand the substantial benefits of the British connection. Men whose business kept them in frequent correspondence with firms in London and whose profits often depended upon the fluctuations of the British markets were far less likely to hold an entirely provincial view of the world about them than those whose direct contacts were wholly local. A colonial merchant was apt to be at least a little better posted about changes in London fashions, about British political gossip, or about the prospects of war or peace than was the colonist who, if he cared at all, depended for his information simply on rumor or the meager items in the colonial newspaper. And the colonial shipper, who relied on London for marine insurance and on British diplomatic agencies and the British Navy for the protection of his ventures, was far more likely to value his position as a British subject than the colonial farmer, who never saw a British frigate, or a simple fisherman, who saw it only to fear its press gang. The colonial merchant might dislike and try to evade some of the restrictions placed by Parliament on the freedom of his trade; he might object actively and even forcefully to measures which smacked too much of favoritism to British or West India interests. But more than any other American not a government official the colonial merchant was aware that the colonies were a part of the British world and dependent on the mother country for their protection and for much of their prosperity. Unlike the frontiersman, to whom Europe was very distant both in place and time, the merchant felt it still very much a part of his daily life.[19]

[19] In *The Colonial Merchants and the American Revolution, 1763–1776* (New York: Columbia University Press, 1918), p. 31, Arthur M. Schlesinger quotes a letter from a merchants' committee of Philadelphia to a similar group in London, November 25, 1769: "We consider the merchants here and in England as the links of the chain that binds both countries together. They are deeply concerned in preserving the union

Colonial merchants tended to be conservative, finally, because their business demanded stability. A sudden shift in the basis of taxation, a disturbance of the domestic market in consequence of local legislation, a drop in the productivity of the laboring classes because of political or religious excitement, or a sharp change in the value of money could, then as now, cause the businessman anxiety, trouble, and loss. Most branches of trade could best be conducted if changes in the underlying conditions of community life came slowly and only under the guidance of the businessman himself. Hence in all questions affecting the internal economy of the colonies the colonial merchant normally used his influence on the side of stability and the maintenance of the accustomed order of affairs.

No single domestic issue so generally engaged the attention of the merchants throughout the colonies as did that of the currency; in the whole range of American history, national as well as colonial, no public questions have more consistently epitomized the conflict of interest between economic groups than have those which dealt with the medium of exchange. In the history of our Federal Government the subject has arisen again and again in one form or another from the time of Alexander Hamilton's financial program, through the wildcat banking era of Jackson's day, the greenback controversies of the post-Civil War decade, and the silver-coinage disputes of the later nineteenth century, to the monetary policies of the New Deal. Regardless of the particular form in which the question has arisen, it has usually found the Westerner (whatever might constitute the "West" at any given moment), the farmer, and the debtor generally arrayed in favor of cheap currency and looking with a friendly eye upon any project that has an inflationary tend-

---

and connection." The letter was printed in the London *Chronicle*, March 3, 1770, and in *The Pennsylvania Gazette*, May 10, 1770.

ency. The Easterner, the commercial groups, and the creditor class have usually been advocates of "sound money" and of a medium of exchange definitely restricted in amount and sustained in value. The fundamental issues and the grouping of opposing forces have remained unchanged whatever the specific program under discussion.

The battles over currency in our national history have been essentially a continuation of a conflict begun in colonial times. Colonial farmers, frontiersmen, and the debtor class as a whole urged the issuance of large amounts of legal-tender paper currency in nearly all the colonies. The wealthier inhabitants of the urban centers, merchants, and creditors generally sought to curtail such issues in order to keep a stable currency and avoid the dangers of unrestrained inflation.

The colonial struggles over the monetary medium differed from those of the national period in two significant respects. First, legal-tender paper currency was issued by as many different governments as there were colonies, instead of by a single central authority. The battle was therefore fought afresh in each colony, though the decisions reached in one province might seriously affect conditions in a neighbor. Since the quantities of paper issued, the terms of redemption, and the credit of the issuing government varied greatly from colony to colony, the emissions differed widely in value. The result was a confusion that complicated business transactions, especially across colonial boundaries, to a degree never duplicated in the national period, except conceivably at the height of wildcat banking in Jackson's time. Second, the most vigorous opposition to proposals for expanding the colonial currency and making it legal tender did not come from within America at all but from British merchants and the British government. These merchants felt the adverse effects of a depreciated colonial currency and experienced none of its benefits. Officials of the home government often understood little or nothing of the actual conditions that called forth colonial monetary legislation, but they did understand their merchants' complaints and regularly sought to protect them. From the royal proclamation of 1704 and the Coinage Act of 1707, through a series of instructions to governors and disallowances of colonial laws, to the New England Currency Act of 1751 and the final Act of 1764 forbidding legal-tender bills of credit in all the colonies, the British government fought a continuous battle for "sound money" in the colonies in the interest, chiefly, of the British merchants.

British merchants and the home government that almost always supported them tried their best to prevent all emission of paper money in the colonies. Colonial merchants, on the other hand, were in a different position. Although quite as anxious, usually, as their British correspondents that the monetary system be kept on a sound basis, they understood the local conditions which made some substitute for gold and silver absolutely essential. The English colonies had no mines of the precious metals, and what specie they had came almost entirely from trade with other parts of the New World. In the colonies as a whole and during most of the period, imports from Great Britain generally exceeded exports to the mother country, and the foreign coin regularly flowed out in payment of the adverse balance. Consequently, the colonists had no adequate metallic currency. Although some commodity money was used, such as tobacco in Virginia and Maryland, there was no comparable medium outside the staple colonies that could begin to serve adequately the needs of a growing commerce and a large and scattered population. Colonial merchants, who daily faced the perplexities which this scarcity of currency produced, recognized the necessity for some artificial or fiat money and so usually favored a limited issue of paper bills of credit. At the same time, most of them understood the dangers of depreciation and inflation and consequently took a moderate position, opposing alike the colonial extremists who would flood the land with legal-tender bills and the British government which would prohibit them entirely.

This realistic position of the colonial businessman was well expressed by John Watts, a leading merchant of New York, in a letter to a London friend written soon after the parliamentary act of 1764 which finally forbade the issue of any legal-tender bills of credit in colonial America. "The use of paper money is abolished as an evil," he wrote, "when, properly treated, it is the only medium we have left of commerce and the only expedient in an exigency. Every man of estate here abominates the abuse of paper money, because the consequences fall upon himself, but there is just the same difference in the use and abuse of it as there is in food itself, or in every one necessary convenience or pleasure of life."[20]

While men like Watts recognized the need for a colonial paper currency and objected only to its abuse, a few extreme conservatives opposed the idea entirely. Judge Samuel Sewall of Boston was one of those who could see nothing but evil in any kind of fiat money. A medium of exchange should have intrinsic worth, he felt, and government credit seemed to the skeptical old gentleman too unreliable a foundation for a system of currency. "If money be wanting," he wrote in 1712, "'twere a better expedient to oblige creditors to take wheat, Indian corn, salt, iron, wool at a moderate valuation, as 'twas of old: then there would be *quid pro quo*; whereas now private creditors are forced to take the public faith for payment for their commodity."[21] Some others shared Sewall's doubts of the reliability of public credit, and it must be admitted that experience in several

[20] *Letter Book of John Watts*, pp. 348–49.
[21] *Diary of Samuel Sewall, 1674–1729* (Collections of the Massachusetts Historical Society, 5th Series, V–VII, Boston, 1878–82), II, 366.

colonies gave grounds for their skepticism. Colonial legislatures succumbed all too often to the temptation to postpone a redemption date or to increase the emission of paper beyond the actual needs of business simply as a means of paying government expenses instead of imposing unpopular taxation.

But most opponents of large emissions of paper currency based their objections on two other grounds, one primarily social, the other economic. On the one hand, large issues of paper money led to extravagance and luxury, especially among the common people, for whom, as their richer neighbors were apt to feel, plain living was the proper way of life. On the other hand, the depreciation that usually followed the emission of large sums of legal-tender bills made it possible for debtors to pay off their debts at rates which cheated creditors of their just dues. These two objections are suggested in an anonymous letter to the Boston *News-Letter* in 1735:

> Paper money is the reproach and scandal of our province; *first*, for that whereas we had originally a silver currency among us, we have extravagantly squandered it away in purchasing foreign commodities, which we ought either *industriously* to have produced and manufactured ourselves, or (if that was not to be done) frugally to have lived without 'em; *secondly*, for that it has made us dishonest in the payment of our debts, both at home and abroad, to the great dishonor and infamy of our country. Have we not, therefore, more need of sumptuary laws to restrain our vanity and extravagance than of new emissions of paper to encourage it? [22]

The social argument against currency inflation was further developed by a New Jersey writer in 1768. "The extreme plenty of money, in the latter part of the late war," he stated, "hath proved the greatest mischief that ever happened to these provinces. It relaxed industry, promoted idleness, encouraged run-

[22] *Boston Weekly News-Letter*, February 28–March 7, 1734 [1735 n.s.], No. 1570.

ning into debt, opened a door to profusion and high living, luxury, and excess of every kind." The author was sure "that the most superficial observer must be surprised at the difference in living and dress between 1755 and the present time, besides the expensive diversions, and scenes of dissipation, unknown among us till of late; and now the ebb tide not floating us where we used to swim, it occasions loud complaints, charging all our distresses to the scarcity of cash." To attribute the existing distress to a scarcity of money was wholly unsound, he declared; New Jersey's paper currency had jumped from £20,000 in 1754 to nearly £220,000 in 1768; Pennsylvania's circulation had increased fourfold. Frugality was the solution of the country's troubles. As a starter in a campaign of self-denial he proposed that New Jersey and Pennsylvania do without tea: these two provinces alone could save £200,000 by this one expedient.[23]

The greatest objection to unlimited paper money and the one that chiefly called forth the opposition of colonial merchants and other members of the creditor class was the effect of inflation upon prices and outstanding debts. To the farmer and the debtor a steadily depreciating currency seemed most desirable, for it enabled the one to sell his produce at ever-increasing prices and the other to discharge his debts at a real value far less than that which he had originally contracted to pay. But the merchant found the situation just the reverse. Like all members of the creditor class he found the sums due him ultimately paid in a depreciated currency and considered himself defrauded. That such men felt keenly about the situation and tried to do some-

[23] The letter, dated "Hunterdon, West Jersey, Jan. 7, 1768," and the accompanying essay from which these quotations have been taken are printed in *New Jersey Archives*, 1st Series, XXVI (Paterson, N.J.: The Call Printing and Publishing Co., 1904), 5–8. My attention was called to them by extracts given in Donald L. Kemmerer, *Path to Freedom; The Struggle for Self-Government in Colonial New Jersey, 1703–1776* (Princeton: Princeton University Press, 1940), pp. 303–4.

thing about it to their advantage is evident not only in the legislative history of the various colonies, where bitter contests over monetary matters are recorded, but also in the pages of the colonial newspapers, where again and again the spokesmen of the creditor class called on the public for fair play.

A communication in the Boston *News-Letter* in 1736 is characteristic. The writer asserted that probably more than three quarters of the people in the province were debtors. Most of them seemed to be doing all they could to lessen instead of improve the value of the current bills, "very much to the loss and damage of the fair trader. How many men have got estates by the fall of our money, and consequently goods rising upon their hands, which they were long in debt for, I cannot tell. But it is very apparent that a great many have and what they have got that way it is pretty plain others have lost, which deserves no softer a name than that of a notorious cheat. And how can we expect a blessing on our affairs carried on in this manner I know not."[24]

Thus the colonial merchant, while far from being as extreme on the question as was his British counterpart, nevertheless generally set himself against the efforts of the debtor class to bring about a currency inflation. In the ensuing battles he was generally and characteristically enrolled on the conservative side. He did not always win. In Rhode Island, for example, where the radical element was strongest, the most conservative merchants of Newport were in a small minority, and the inflation of the currency there became a subject of reproach in all the neighboring colonies. In some colonies he was more successful. The outstanding example of a merchant who led his fellow conservatives to victory on the currency question was Thomas Hutchinson of Massachusetts. He had long opposed the infla-

[24] *Boston Weekly News-Letter*, February 26–March 4, 1736 [1737 n.s.], No. 1672.

tionary tendencies in the Bay Colony and declared himself effectively in favor of a "hard-money" policy in a pamphlet published in 1736. His great chance came in 1748 when the British government sent over about £183,000 to repay Massachusetts for her expenditures in the Louisbourg campaign. Hutchinson proposed that the colony use the specie, not to reduce its current taxes, but to call in and retire its badly depreciated bills of credit at a rate of eleven for one. The fight was bitter and cost Hutchinson his seat in the assembly. But he won out in the end and from that time forward Massachusetts was able to boast a currency as sound as that in any of her neighboring colonies. In few of the achievements of his long and active life did Hutchinson take a more lasting pride. And he in turn came to be regarded as the archetype and leader of the conservative merchants of New England.[25]

Among the economic groups in colonial America, the landed gentry on their great plantations or country estates and the merchants in their countinghouses were the most effective bulwarks against radical change. It was to the interest of both groups to oppose the growing spirit of liberalism, whether it came from frontier farmers or from the unenfranchised artisans of the towns. How valuable such conservatives, especially the great planters, might be to the British interest was pointed out by Governor Tryon of North Carolina and New York shortly before the Revolution.

"I conceive it, my Lord," he wrote to Secretary of State Hillsborough, "good policy to lodge large tracts of land in the hands of gentlemen of weight and consideration. They will

[25] Hutchinson's own accounts of this affair are to be found in Thomas Hutchinson, *The History of the Colony and Province of Massachusetts-Bay*, edited by Lawrence Shaw Mayo (Cambridge: Harvard University Press, 1936), II, 333–37, and in Hutchinson, *Diary and Letters*, I, 49–54.

naturally farm out their lands to tenants, a method which will ever create subordination, and counterpoise, in some measure, the general leveling spirit that so much prevails in some of His Majesty's governments."[26] It was to the interest of the planters and merchants to preserve the *status quo*, politically, economically, and socially; and, in spite of conflicts, they generally succeeded in maintaining their authority throughout the colonial period. They controlled the instruments of local government and, to a large extent, were backed by the British authorities. The lowest class of colonists were landless and had no vote; the yeomen farmers and the mechanics were unorganized and lacked effective leadership. As long as such conditions continued, the conservative leaders might feel reasonably secure in power.

But the approach of the Revolution offered a twofold threat to their position, though most of them failed at first to recognize the dual nature of the danger. On the one hand, the new British policies seemed to challenge from the outside their control of local government and to threaten their economic security and advancement. The new taxes and the narrower control of commerce hurt the merchants seriously and directly. Some of the planters were interested in western lands, primarily as a speculation, as we have seen, and they feared that British interests in these regions were being advanced at their expense. A few, perhaps, saw in rebellion an opportunity to repudiate their debts to British merchants, as the Tory parson of Maryland, Jonathan Boucher, charged. But for the majority more fundamental issues than these were at stake. By one means or another, chiefly through control of finance, the local political leaders had reduced the actual power of the royal governor to a fraction of what it was on paper. But, recently made restless by British interference with local legislation, as in the disallowance of Vir-

[26] *N. Y. Col. Docs.*, VIII, 293 .

ginia monetary laws which led up to the Parson's Cause in 1763, they were concerned lest parliamentary taxation take from themselves that control of finance which was so all-important to the exercise of self-government.

In a sense, the planters' and merchants' resistance to British authority was an expression of a conservative attitude, in spite of the fact that it led in time to open rebellion. These men wanted to preserve the *status quo*, which, generally speaking, favored their interests and their control of local affairs. British policy after 1763 involved a series of innovations which threatened that control. It constituted a danger, therefore, which a large proportion of the colonial ruling class felt they ought to oppose. That resistance might lead in time to extremes and that it would be accompanied by the development of another and internal danger to the security of their class was a possibility that many of them failed to appreciate until too late.

The other threat came from the underprivileged classes in the colonies themselves. Resistance to authority, however limited its objective and conservative its leadership, is dangerous for the very example it sets. It may call into being extralegal weapons and agreements for the sole purpose of evading or defeating a particular measure of government. But matters do not necessarily stop there. Other men may use this example of resistance and the weapons it has produced to attack other forms of authority that were quite acceptable to those who first invoked the principle. So it was during the revolutionary years in America. The local aristocracy, in opposing the growth of British authority from without, opened the way for the lower classes to oppose the authority and the privileges which the colonial leaders had long maintained at home. What was equally important, the period of agitation produced for the first time in a hundred years men who were able to speak for the common people and lead them in their attack upon entrenched privilege.

Men like Thomas Jefferson, Samuel Adams, and Patrick Henry used the troubled times and the general impairment of authority to press for greater equality among the people of the colonies. The internal danger to the position of the aristocracy was thus quite as great as the external.

The dual nature of the threat at last became apparent. In opposing danger from without, the conservatives had helped to bring on a fresh danger from within. Some few drew back from further resistance to Great Britain in the face of the internal threat. Others were too deeply and sincerely committed to the American cause to follow suit. Some tried to ride out the storm, hoping against hope that somehow both dangers might be averted and their class regain its former position of political and social authority. Such a one was Landon Carter of Virginia. In the early days of the agitation he had been a stanch opponent of British authority and later indirectly claimed credit for having introduced in 1764 the Virginia resolutions usually attributed to Patrick Henry, which, as Carter wrote, "gave the first breath of liberty in America." But by the time men were seriously discussing independence, Carter's fears were aroused. A republic was just as dangerous as a monarchy, he thought, and in an independent state "we might fall into a worse situation from internal oppression and commotions than might have been obtained by a serious as well as a cautious reconciliation."[27] It was men like Patrick Henry whom he feared most, as did many of his fellow planters. Any news that would lessen his fears of Henry was good news. And so July 13, 1776, seemed at the time to be a red-letter day to Carter, for it brought word of events equally ominous to British monarchy, represented by the royal governor, Lord Dunmore, and to American republicanism in the

[27] "Diary of Colonel Landon Carter," *William and Mary Quarterly*, 1st Series, XVII (July 1909), 39, 44; XX (January 1912), 184–86; XXI (January 1913), 178.

person of the new state governor, Patrick Henry. Even though one item of this news later proved to have been mere wishful thinking on somebody's part, Carter's diary entry is well worth repeating since it epitomizes better than any other contemporary writing the attitude of many an aristocrat in the face of the double threat to his security which the Revolution implied. A visitor arrived after dinner that day, Carter wrote joyfully, bringing a report from Hampton "that Patrick Henry, the late-elected governor, died last Tuesday evening. So that being the day of our batteries' beginning to play on Dunmore's gang and they being routed, we ought to look on those two joined as two glorious events, particularly favorable by the hand of Providence."[28] Of course, Patrick Henry was not dead as Carter and his guest supposed. But for the moment the planter aristocrat was happy. The routing of the royal governor and his "gang" and the death of the radical patriot governor: to a man of Carter's position and heritage it would be hard to say which would contribute more to a restoration of provincial society as he had always known it and to the continued supremacy of his own class. For that restoration and that supremacy were the natural objectives of the planter and the merchant, as representatives of colonial conservatism.

[28] *Ibid.*, XX (January 1912), 184.

3

PULPIT AND BROADCLOTH

"My son, fear thou the Lord and the king: and meddle not with them that are given to change."[1] This Biblical admonition, which served as a text for more than one sermon in the American colonies,[2] sums up the attitude of many of the colonial ministers on issues of their day. The church may be a liberalizing, vitalizing power in society; but the church, especially an organized and established Church, may also be a conservative, even reactionary, force. Both characteristics were present in the religious organizations of the American colonies, but our present concern is with the conservative side of colonial religion. We shall devote our attention primarily to the attitudes and actions of those churchmen who, in the words of one of them, felt called upon "to stand up for the *good old Way*, and bear faithful testimony against everything that may tend to cast a blemish on *true primitive* Christianity."[3]

[1] Proverbs 24:21.

[2] For example, Isaac Stiles, *A Prospect of the City of Jerusalem in It's Spiritual Building, Beauty and Glory, Showed in a Sermon Preached at Hartford at the Election . . . . May 13, 1742* (New London, Conn., 1742), p. 57; and Jonathan Boucher, "On Reducing the Revenue of the Clergy" (preached in 1771), printed in his *A View of the Causes and Consequences of the American Revolution; in Thirteen Discourses, Preached in North America between the Years 1763 and 1775: with an Historical Preface* (London, 1797), pp. 202–40. (This collection of Boucher's sermons will hereafter be cited as Boucher, *American Revolution.*)

[3] Charles Chauncy, *Seasonable Thoughts on the State of Religion in New-England* (Boston, 1743), pp. 336–37. The italics are Chauncy's.

Eight or ten Christian denominations had enough followers in eighteenth-century America to play significant parts in the religious life of the English colonies. Among them, the Anglicans, Puritans (New England Congregationalists), Presbyterians, and Quakers were undoubtedly the most numerous and, in different localities, the most influential. But only two organized churches attained the privileged position of full and legal establishment in any of the Continental colonies: the Anglican Church in the Southern Colonies and to a limited extent in New York,[4] and the Puritan or Congregational Church in Massachusetts and Connecticut. While other denominations might exist side by side in such a colony as Pennsylvania, with complete liberty if not always with complete good will, these two established churches, each in its own area, looked on all others as interlopers, to be tolerated if necessary, but not to be accorded any greater freedom than the law absolutely required. Their preferred position, as well as their history and their doctrines, tended to make the Anglican and the Puritan churches the most conservative of all the organized religious bodies in the colonies.

In communities where these churches were established their spokesmen usually held that widespread sectarianism was a violation of all principles of decency and order, a definitely antisocial phenomenon. The New England Puritans had founded their colonies with the aim of establishing a "New Zion," a community where God's children, freed from the corrupting influence of the Anglican hierarchy and insulated from the heretical notions of Anabaptists, Quakers, and other radicals, could recreate the true Church in purity of form and soundness of doctrine. As time went on, such an ideal church-state proved impossible to maintain. Not only did Anglicans win a slender foot-

---

[4] In New York, both the Anglican and the Dutch Reformed Churches enjoyed some of the privileges of establishment, but neither to the complete exclusion of the other.

hold in the citadel of their strongest opponents, but sectaries of various breeds also crept in. Circumstances forced the upholders of the established Puritan Church to grant these "enemies of truth" some measure of toleration. But their presence was a menace to Christian society. As Isaac Stiles, a Connecticut pastor, said of the Separatists in an election sermon, their transactions were "a great blemish to the Christian name and profession, directly contrary to St. Paul's rule *Let all things be done decently and in order*." Such men, Stiles said, "are subversive of *peace, discipline, and government*, lay open the sluices, and make a gap to let in a flood of confusion and disorder, and very awfully portend the ruin of these churches." If sectarianism increased, Connecticut "would soon be *an habitation of dragons and a court for owls*."[5] The hyperbole of Stiles's language may perhaps be forgiven if one recognizes his sincerity. To an orthodox Puritan no warning could be too strongly put when danger threatened both church and state.

Anglicans everywhere felt much the same way about nonconformists. They had the additional belief that their Church, being the only one among English-speaking Protestant bodies founded on the principle of Apostolic Succession, was alone a historically valid church. Dissenting ministers were, of course, not truly ordained, and the "republican" or "democratic" governments of many dissenting sects were a perversion of sound church organization and discipline. Expressions of scorn for dissenters came not only from men living in colonies where the Anglican Church was established but from others also. The Reverend Richard Peters, writing to the Archbishop of Canterbury from Philadelphia in 1763, described the Presbyterians in unflattering terms. Their ministers, he pointed out especially, were in general "men of small talents and mean education," wholly subservient to their congregations, "who either starve

[5] Stiles, *A Prospect of the City of Jerusalem*, p. 58.

them, or whenever they take a dislike, though for just exercise
of the ministerial influence, they turn them off." Yet ministers
as well as laymen were "fond to a madness of these popular
forms of government and would dislike bishops on any footing."[6] The republicanism of the dissenters, according to Anglicans, carried over into the political field and tended to undermine the civil state. Thus Lieutenant Governor Colden of New
York, writing about the land riots of the 1760's, declared that
the troublemakers consisted chiefly of dissenters, the most active among them being "independents from New England or
educated there, and of republican principles."[7] As late as the
close of the Revolution, an Anglican divine of Delaware wrote
back to England denouncing the nonconformists, especially the
"ignorant Methodists and Anabaptists, some of whose absurd-
ities has as direct a tendency to overturn all order and decency
in the Church, as the base principles and practices of those who
call themselves Whigs (a soft term for rebels) have in the state."[8]

Of all the Anglicans in colonial America the Reverend Jonathan Boucher made the most vigorous attack on dissenters.
Boucher had come to Virginia as a young man to act as tutor in
a planter's family. Later he had made a trip to England to
receive Holy Orders and then held successively parishes in Virginia and Maryland. At the outbreak of the Revolution he
was rector of Queen Anne's Parish in St. George's County,
Maryland. An ardent churchman and a stanch Loyalist, he was
altogether the most emphatic and prolific spokesman for a conservative and even reactionary point of view anywhere in the
Southern Colonies.[9] In a sermon on "Schisms and Sects"

[6] Perry, *Historical Collections*, III, 393.

[7] *Colden Letter Books*, II, 211; *N. Y. Col. Docs.*, VIII, 208.

[8] Perry, *Historical Collections*, V, 139.

[9] Boucher's ardent conservatism reveals itself not only in his collected sermons but also in his autobiography, *Reminiscences of an
American Loyalist, 1738–1789, Being the Autobiography of the Revd.*

preached in 1769 he gave utterance to his opinion of "these sectaries of our western world." He cited St. Paul, who had described them "as persons having 'itching ears' and 'unstable in all their ways,' and who are therefore 'easily tossed about with every wind of doctrine.'" Some churchmen, he admitted, would let these schismatics go their way, believing that they were too insignificant to do any harm. But Boucher declared that this was not "a case in which there can be any neutrality! Those who are not for the Church are against it." A sect, he believed, was, in fact, "a revolt against the authority of the Church, just as a faction is against the authority of the State; or, in other words, a sect is a faction in the Church, as a faction is a sect in the State; and the spirit which refuses obedience to the one is equally ready to resist the other." It followed, therefore, that all laws curbing the dissenting sects must be rigidly enforced if "institutions and regulations which were of great moment to the welfare of society" were not to be weakened and ultimately destroyed.[10]

A peculiar situation developed in New England when the Anglican Church began to make inroads into Massachusetts and Connecticut, areas which the Puritans had settled and had marked out as their own. Both churches were essentially conservative in their views, but conservative in different ways. The Anglicans looked back to an English background, they contended that the Established Church of the mother country ought to have at least equal privileges with any other denomination in an English colony, and they criticized the political and religious organizations of the Puritan colonies as dangerously

---

Jonathan Boucher, Rector of Annapolis in Maryland and Afterwards Vicar of Epsom, Surrey, England, edited by his grandson, Jonathan Bouchier (Boston and New York: Houghton Mifflin Company, 1925) (hereafter cited as Boucher, *Reminiscences*).

[10] Boucher, *American Revolution,* pp. 46–88, especially pp. 77–80.

"republican" and "democratic." The Puritans, on the other hand, viewed the Anglicans as interlopers. They reminded themselves that their forefathers had fled from the persecutions of Archbishop Laud and had founded these colonies in order to be free from interference by the Anglican hierarchy. The intrusion of Anglican "missionaries" and the establishment of Anglican churches in the heart of New England seemed to threaten the "established order" the Puritans had so painfully created. Granted that the Anglicans were neither heretics nor radicals, they were nonetheless a constant menace to the *status quo*. In 1722 Timothy Cutler resigned as rector of stanchly orthodox Yale College and with Samuel Johnson went to England for episcopal ordination. Upon their return Cutler became rector of Christ Church, Boston, and Johnson became minister of the first Anglican church in Connecticut at Stratford. This was a triumph for the Church of England, but orthodox Puritans felt the same way about Cutler and Johnson that patriotic Norwegians of 1940 felt about Quisling.[11] An attitude of suspicion and dislike of the Anglicans persisted in many quarters of New England throughout the eighteenth century.

The Anglicans, on their part, looked upon the New England system with something approaching scorn. The Congregational ministers, lacking episcopal ordination, were not true clergymen at all, they thought. In Massachusetts the Anglicans for years consistently referred to them by the disrespectful term of "dissenting teachers." In spite of remonstrances from as high a

---

[11] Two Yale trustees characterized Cutler's defection as "a foul frustration of the confidence reposed in him," and another writer described his acceptance of the rectorship of Yale at a time when his beliefs were already veering over to Anglicanism as a move which "gave him an opportunity privately to destroy the principal intention of the academy, and blow up the churches which he appeared a friend to." Franklin B. Dexter, *Documentary History of Yale University* (New Haven: Yale University Press, 1916), pp. 228–30.

quarter as Lieutenant Governor Dummer, the phrase stuck, at least in correspondence among the Anglicans themselves, and Timothy Cutler went so far, in a private letter, as to refer to the Congregational churches of Massachusetts as "conventicles." The church into which Cutler had been born and in which he was first ordained was no longer, in his opinion, a church at all.[12]

The Anglican clergy of Connecticut particularly disliked the governmental system of the colony established by its charter. Samuel Johnson, for over thirty years rector at Stratford, wrote to the Archbishop of Canterbury in 1760, soon after his removal to New York to become president of King's College, that Connecticut was potentially a fine colony: "for its bigness it is the best of all His Majesty's colonies in America." But it had a nearly fatal drawback. "All the disadvantages it labors under are owing to its wretched constitution, being little more than a mere democracy, and most of them upon a level, and each man thinking himself an able divine and politician; hence the prevalence of rigid enthusiasms and conceited notions and practices in religion, and republican and mobbish principles and practices, next door to anarchy, in polity." Again and again during his ministry in the colony, this son of Connecticut urged that its charter be revoked. The Congregationalists, he wrote, three years after assuming his Stratford rectorship, "all boast themselves an establishment, and look down upon the poor Church of England with contempt, as a despicable, schismatical, and popish communion; and their charter is, indeed, the foundation of all their insolence. Happy would it be for the Church of England if it were taken away." The Congregational Church polity seemed just as bad as the civil government. Even before his conversion to Anglicanism, as Johnson later wrote in his autobiography, he had taken a dislike to the congregational form of church government, "in which every brother has a hand,

[12] Perry, *Historical Collections*, III, 206–65.

which . . . . he plainly saw tended too much to conceit and self-sufficiency and to endless feuds, censoriousness, and unchari-tableness. . . . . He was convinced that a way so entirely popular could but very poorly and he thought not long subsist, to answer any ends of government, but must from the nature of it crumble to pieces as every individual seemed to think himself infallible." To the twentieth-century American mind, the Connecticut system of Johnson's time seems oligarchical and conservative enough. But to Johnson and to others like him—though there were few so distinguished and none so able among New England Anglicans as he—the "democratic" traits of Connecticut polity in church and civil state were dangerously advanced and radical.[13]

Both established churches were faced with the problem of religious toleration. By the beginning of the eighteenth century, most leaders of both denominations had come to recognize that complete suppression of dissent was no longer possible, even if it were desirable. In every colony, either by tacit consent or by

[13] Francis L. Hawks and William S. Perry, eds., *Documentary History of the Protestant Episcopal Church, in the United States of America, Containing Numerous Hitherto Unpublished Documents Concerning the Church in Connecticut* (New York, 1863–64), I, 111, 312 (hereafter cited as Hawks and Perry, *Documentary History*); Herbert and Carol Schneider, eds., *Samuel Johnson, President of King's College: His Career and Writings* (New York: Columbia University Press, 1929), I, 295. Compare Johnson's views on democracy in Church and State with the assertion of John Wise of Ipswich, Mass., "That a democracy in church or state is a very honorable and regular government according to the dictates of right reason. And therefore . . . . that these churches of New England, in their ancient constitution of church order, it being a democracy, are manifestly justified and defended by the law and light of nature." *A Vindication of the Government of New England Churches* (Boston, 1717), pp. 67–68. This passage is quoted and discussed in Alice M. Baldwin, *The New England Clergy and the American Revolution* (Durham: Duke University Press, 1928), pp. 28–29.

formal legislation, independent religious groups won the right to organize and hold church services, though their members might still be taxed to support the established ministry.

But that the governments of these colonies were willing to permit some nonconformists to worship according to their own consciences did not mean that the more conservative members of the established churches were ready to grant complete religious liberty. There was a limit to the freedom which dissenters ought to have. Standing instructions to the governors of all royal provinces directed them "to permit a liberty of conscience to all persons except Papists, so they be contented with a quiet and peaceable enjoyment of the same, not giving offense or scandal to the government."[14] Such an order left a good deal of latitude for interpretation. In the middle of the century the General Court of Virginia licensed seven meetinghouses in five counties for Presbyterian worship under one itinerant preacher, Samuel Davies. In all these five counties there were only eight ministers of the Anglican Church. William Dawson, commissary of the Bishop of London, wrote his superior in 1750 that it seemed to him quite excessive indulgence had been granted Davies, especially as "several of the laiety as well as clergy" were "uneasy on account of the countenance and encouragement he has met with." Dawson himself was concerned "to see schism spreading itself through a colony that has been famous for uniformity of religion."[15]

Jonathan Boucher, somewhat later, was equally disturbed by the number of sectaries in Virginia. "I might almost as well pretend to count the gnats that buzz around us in a summer's evening," he asserted from the pulpit. "Like gnats, moreover,

[14] In Maryland to 1703, and in other provinces during the reign of James II, the words "except Papists" were omitted. Toleration of Roman Catholics was also prescribed in the instructions for Nova Scotia and the territories won in 1763. Labaree, *Royal Instructions*, II, 494–502.

[15] Perry, *Historical Collections*, I, 366.

the noise which sectaries make not only disturbs and is disagreeable, but we find that, though they can neither give pleasure nor do any good, they do not want either the disposition or the ability of those little insignificant animals to tease, to sting, and to torment."[16] On the very eve of the Revolution, he preached a sermon in Maryland "On the Toleration of Papists" in which he pointed out that the most celebrated political writers of all ages and countries had agreed that "many and great evils" would arise from a state's giving equal countenance to all religions indiscriminately. "Equally fatal to the religion and the morals of the people would be the introduction of that visionary project of some rash theorists in whose ideal states no preference should be shown to any particular system of religion." Such a scheme would inevitably bring a relaxation of principle and give countenance to systems unfavorable to good morals and "sometimes (it may be) to systems hostile to the very state by which they are supported and destructive of all civil authority."[17]

Conservative New England Puritans felt much as did the Anglican leaders about religious liberty, but their spokesman placed the emphasis rather more strongly on the protection of the Established Church and its supporters from outside interference. William Worthington, pastor at Saybrook, Connecticut, pointed out in an election sermon in 1744 that the Church, "as a politic body," had temporal interests, respecting which

[16] Boucher, "On the American Episcopate," *American Revolution*, p. 100.

[17] Boucher, "On the Toleration of Papists," *ibid*, pp. 259–61. In a footnote to this passage in the 1797 edition of these sermons Boucher referred to the recent adoption by most of the new American States of the "visionary project" of complete disestablishment "which might have been supposed too wild even for modern politics to have thought of." He thought the scheme had already proved "to be of the utmost danger to real religion" and proceeded to paint a dismal picture of the future of religion in America.

she had "as good a right to the rulers' care as any embodied society." Some people, he admitted, were disposed "to deny the magistrate any right to make laws about, or take cognizance of, religious affairs, as if every man had a good right to follow his conscience how dreadfully soever it errs, a valuable privilege he ought not to suffer an encroachment upon in the least." But, as the Old Testament makes clear, God gave laws circumscribing conscience and forbidding the Jews to worship idols, and modern society should follow this divine example.[18]

Thus both Anglican and Puritan conservatives were willing to give lip service to the principle of religious liberty, yet they so hedged this freedom about with "ifs" and "buts" in the interest of their established churches, of society as they thought it ought to be, and of the truth as they specifically saw it, that the privilege they were willing to grant to others became in fact merely a limited toleration of dissent and not a complete freedom for all religious faith and practice.

The Anglican Church stood in a special position among American denominations because it was the established church, not only of certain colonies, but of the mother country as well. Throughout the colonies the clergymen of this denomination served as an important connecting link between the religious and cultural life of England and that of her transatlantic settlements. To the regret of the most zealous churchmen in America, the home government never saw fit to authorize the consecration of a resident bishop for the colonies. Instead, the churches and their clergymen were under the general jurisdiction of the Bishop of London.[19] The absence of a resident bishop in America

[18] William Worthington, *The Duty of Rulers and Teachers in Unitedly Leading God's People, Urged & Explained* (New London, 1744), pp. 10–11.

[19] The standard account of the controversies over the appointment of a colonial bishop is Arthur L. Cross, *The Anglican Episcopate and the American Colonies* (New York: Longmans, Green and Company

meant that no priests could be ordained here, since, of course, in this Church only a bishop has the power to ordain. Consequently, every clergyman who served in the colonies had to be a native of the British Isles, ordained there before his departure for America, or else a colonial who had taken the long, expensive, and often hazardous voyage to England to receive ordination at the hands of a bishop before entering upon his priestly office in the colonies. Of no other colonial church could it be said that every minister was either a native of Great Britain or had been there at least once during his lifetime. Indeed, it would be impossible to say as much of any other single group of individuals, clerical or lay, in all the English colonies, even including the royal governors.

Another agency that played a considerable part in fostering the tie between the colonial and the English churches was the Society for the Propagation of the Gospel in Foreign Parts, often referred to as the "Venerable Society," and more familiarly known as the "S.P.G." It was particularly active in financing the work of missionaries in those northern colonies where Anglicanism was weakest. It also provided small libraries and a few teachers in places where reading and education under Church auspices seemed likely to be most helpful. The Church of England would have made slow progress indeed in southern New England and in parts of the Middle Colonies had it not been for the financial support of the S.P.G. Thus it can be said not only that every minister of an Anglican church in the colonies had had some period, at least, of residence in Great Britain, but also that the great majority of such churches either were in colonies where Anglicanism was locally established or were dependent

---

1902). See also a useful discussion of the general position of the Church of England in the colonies by Evarts B. Greene, "The Anglican Outlook of the American Colonies in the Early Eighteenth Century," *American Historical Review*, XX (October 1914), 64-85.

on an organization in the mother country for part of their support.

This close tie between the Anglican Church in America and England was a matter of more than passing significance. The eighteenth century was a period in which the colonies were slowly but steadily developing a life and culture of their own. By the early 1700's in most colonies, a second or a third generation had appeared—men and women born in America with no personal recollection of the England from which their forefathers had come. Many of the new settlers in the later years of the seventeenth and the first years of the eighteenth century were people of non-English stock: Germans, Scots, Scotch-Irish, and some French Huguenots. Although these folk might become faithful subjects, they could not be expected to have the same sentimental feeling about England or be bound to her by the same ties of blood, speech, or religion as native English immigrants. As the century advanced, fewer and fewer of the American colonists had relatives in the mother country with whom they kept up any sort of contact; fewer and fewer, at least proportionately, had any firsthand understanding of what life in England was like. It was true that among the wealthy, the highly educated, and the aristocratic there was a considerable amount of travel back and forth across the Atlantic, and that, as we have observed, the mercantile classes were closely linked by business dealings with the mother country. But as settlement of the interior advanced, as population grew, political maturity increased, and local customs and institutions that had no counterparts in the mother country appeared, these ties with England became more and more fragile. Although they scarcely realized what was happening, the colonists were ceasing to be transplanted Englishmen and were slowly becoming Americans.

When such a trend was under way, any agency or institution

that retained a close link between the colonies and England was of special significance. The Anglican Church provided just such a link. The fact that from the very nature of its organization it could have no permanent existence apart from the hierarchy in Great Britain served as a reminder that it was part of a British institution. However much the members of a parish might cherish their autonomy in local church affairs, they could not escape some contact, direct or indirect, with episcopal authority, if they would be served by any priest at all. However much the smaller congregations of the Northern Colonies preferred financial independence, all too often they found themselves unable to support their ministers without the help—and hence the oversight—of the Society for the Propagation of the Gospel. Whatever the provincialism of their outlook, their restlessness under British control, or their disagreement with British governmental policy, the members of the Anglican Church in America had a place, small though it might be, in the Established Church of England, one of the most important institutions of the mother country.

The effect of this connection was particularly important in the North, where the Anglicans, especially outside New York, were almost always in a small minority. Under the gibes of members of the stronger sects, they sometimes took refuge in the comforting reflection that, after all, they belonged to the official Church of all true Englishmen. Under oppression or persecution, they sought protection not only by the Church at home but by the government which had established it. The connection was strongest of all among the clergy in all the colonies, for their ordination had made them a part of an organization that was very British, and their ordination oaths had placed upon them a special obligation of loyalty to the monarch and obedience to the hierarchy and the government.

As the controversy between the colonies and the mother

country progressed and the cleavage became more and more marked, the Anglican clergy, especially in the North, exerted every effort to preach submission to the state, and to make the Church a bond of union and an effective force for the maintenance of royal authority. As Jonathan Boucher later remarked, with particular reference to Maryland, circumstances and the politicians "had cunningly contrived to place our order in the front of the battle."[20] They were persistent in reminding their congregations, as a Massachusetts Anglican put it, "of the religious obligations and important motives of dutiful respect and submission to the established authority, together with proper confidence in the great wisdom of the government of our parent country. . . . . The influence of this principle has been confessedly observable wherever the Church of England is planted among us."[21]

The Tory doctrine of nonresistance to authority received exposition from many an Anglican pulpit throughout the colonies. The Reverend Dr. George Micklejohn preached such a sermon in 1768 in the presence of Governor Tryon to the North Carolina militia called out to march against the Regulators. He developed his theme from St. Paul's admonition to the Romans:

> Let every soul be subject unto the higher powers. For there is no power but of God: the powers that be are ordained of God.
> Whosoever therefore resisteth the power, resisteth the ordinance of God: and they that resist shall receive to themselves damnation.[22]

Micklejohn argued that resistance to the lawful authority God has set over us could "never possibly be productive of anything

[20] Boucher, *Reminiscences*, p. 69.
[21] Perry, *Historical Collections*, III, 543.
[22] Romans 13:1-2.

but the wildest uproar and most universal confusion." In the last analysis, he warned, "every such wicked and desperate attempt" was "not only treason against an earthly soverign, but rebellion against the most high God." After hearing this sermon no one could be in doubt of his Christian duty in times of civil disturbance, as that duty was expounded by the worthy divine.[23] By such preaching throughout the years of agitation the Anglican clergy justified their contention that they were the great bulwark of authority.

To the other groups which represent a generally conservative attitude in colonial life should be added the two established Churches, Puritan and Anglican. Although there were many men of liberal views, both ministers and laymen, in these as in other denominations, these sects enjoyed privileges in certain colonies which tended to align both churches as institutions and their leaders as individuals in support of the *status quo*.

Differ though they did on many questions of a religious or political nature, the two establishments yet shared certain important attitudes. Spokesmen for both churches expressed a detestation of sectarianism and dissent (including each other in these terms) and did what they could to prevent their spread. Both churches in the eighteenth century gave lip service to the principle of religious toleration, but neither church saw any incongruity in requiring men of other faiths to contribute to the support of the established ministry. And leaders of both used their influence in colonies where they were established to

[23] "On the important Duty of Subjection to the Civil Powers. A Sermon Preached before his Excellency William Tryon, Esquire, ... and the Troops raised to quell the late Insurrection, at Hillsborough, in Orange County, On Sunday September 25, 1768. By Geo. Micklejohn, S.T.D. Newbern: Printed by James Davis, M,DCC,LXVIII"; reprinted in William Boyd, ed., *Some Eighteenth Century Tracts Concerning North Carolina* (Publications of the No. Car. Hist. Commission. Raleigh: Edwards and Broughton Company, 1927).

restrict the toleration granted to others to the least amount consistent with practical necessity and the general spirit of the times. Though such a colony as Pennsylvania had for years offered religious equality to all Christians, though Rhode Island had even granted many privileges to Jews, and though such men as Thomas Jefferson were beginning to advocate the American doctrine of complete separation of Church and State, the Anglican and Puritan leaders held fast to the Old World idea of an established church and deemed themselves generous in acknowledging the right of others simply to worship as they saw fit. In supporting the principle of establishment the Puritans were able to hold out the longer. Although Jefferson's Virginia Statute of Religious Liberty was passed in 1786, it was not until 1818 that Connecticut withdrew the last of the special privileges of the Congregational Church. The Old Guard of Massachusetts did not give up for another fifteen years. Only in 1833 did the last fortress of religious conservatism surrender the principle of establishment under the assaults of a more liberal Americanism.

Nearly a generation before the great political controversies which ushered in the American Revolution, an upheaval took place within the churches themselves which offered to the conservative forces of organized Christianity in all denominations the most vigorous challenge they were to receive during the entire colonial period. After years of comparative calm, a revival occurred which aroused thousands from a state of religious lethargy and self-complacency and led them to a new, more intense, more emotional religious experience than they had ever known before. This Great Awakening, as it was called, was the first large-scale revival in the history of the American churches.[24]

[24] The most useful studies of the Great Awakening are: Joseph Tracy, *The Great Awakening. A History of the Revival of Religion in*

By the end of the seventeenth century, and in some parts of Europe considerably earlier, the flaming religious zeal of the Age of the Reformation had largely burned itself out. Religion still played a part in civil strife, as in the English Revolution of 1688, or in the movement of men from place to place, as in the emigration of French Huguenots after 1685 and the influx of German Pietists to Pennsylvania a little later. But broadly speaking, religion and religious differences were no longer the vital factors they had been; religious fervor became the exception rather than the rule. Great preachers no longer trumpeted a call to crusade for the faith, and when lesser men tried to sound the clarion they were seldom heard above the chorus of more secular appeals to interest and attention. Among the churches of both Europe and America, Protestant Christianity seemed to have lost its militant spirit; worldliness and indifference had crept in to corrupt, if not destroy, the true essence of Christian faith.

The times seemed ripe for a great reaction and a true revival of religion. When it arrived at last it came almost simultaneously in widely scattered parts of Protestant Christendom. First signs seem to have appeared in Germany in the latter part of the seventeenth century. In the 1720's the Dutch Reformed Church of New York began to respond to the appeal of an ardent young preacher, Theodore Frelinghuysen, who summoned his people to a deeper spiritual experience. During the next decade a local revival appeared in and around Northampton, Massachusetts, stimulated by the powerful sermons and personality of Jona-

---

the Time of Edwards and Whitefield (Boston, 1842); Charles H. Maxson, The Great Awakening in the Middle Colonies (Chicago: The University of Chicago Press, [1920]); and W. M. Gewehr, The Great Awakening in Virginia, 1740–1790 (Durham: Duke University Press, 1930), to all three of which I am greatly indebted. There is, however, no single modern work tracing the movement through all the colonies and analyzing its social as well as its religious implications.

than Edwards. At about the same time some of the Presbyterians of Pennsylvania and New Jersey were experiencing a religious quickening under the leadership of graduates of William Tennent's "Log College." Meanwhile, in England the first stirrings of the Methodist revival, under the leadership of John and Charles Wesley, began to be heard, and in Scotland the Kirk was shaken out of its complacency by several Presbyterian divines. By 1740 it was clear that Protestantism was arousing from its slumber.

In its most active phase the Great Awakening in the colonies may be said to date from 1739, when George Whitefield, an early associate of the Wesleys, began his American evangelistic journeys. Calling his hearers from their smugness and their apathy to spiritual experience, he preached the need of true conversion. In a succession of tours between 1739 and 1770, ranging from Georgia to New Hampshire, he aroused thousands to a sense of sin and a quest for personal salvation. Other powerful leaders, such as Edwards, Frelinghuysen, and the Tennents, father and sons, while more restricted in their movements and sometimes more cautious in the emotionalism of their approach, were no less zealous in their appeal for a spiritual rebirth. Very soon a number of lesser preachers began to follow Whitefield's example, many of them making up for what they lacked of his eloquence and personal magnetism by carrying to extremes their emotional appeal and their attack on hostile critics. These itinerants traveled about demanding admission to the pulpits of established ministers, and, as often as not, denouncing their hosts, the regular incumbents, as unregenerate and unfit to preach the Word of God. Some laymen joined in the evangelizing, men completely untrained in theology or homiletics, and making their appeal exclusively to the emotions of their hearers.

The public response to the revivalists was enormous. Many of Whitefield's audiences numbered in the thousands. Uncounted hundreds in every colony were aroused by his preaching, first to a sense of sin, and then, after a period of despair and searching, to a realization of God's grace and an experience of spiritual rebirth. Other evangelists had many converts. Throughout the colonies there was not a denomination, and in the seaboard regions hardly a single church, that was not affected in some degree by the revival movement. In some parishes the great majority of members were won over to the newer emotional approach; in others, the minority, convinced that their fellow members, and often the minister as well, were still in a state of sin, broke away and founded "New Light" or "New Side" churches of their own. To many men the revival seemed not merely an awakening but something approaching a religious revolution as well.

Many conservatives of all denominations, however, looked on the excitement as the work not of God but of the Devil. A number were willing to admit some good in the movement especially in its early days, and to recognize that some genuine conversions were taking place, but they believed that most were merely emotional rather than spiritual experiences and that the evils which the revival brought in its train were far worse than the good it accomplished. It is not my purpose to examine here all the charges which the conservatives brought against the revivalists; nor is our present interest in the inherent truth or falsity of any of their accusations, but in the evidence they reveal of the fundamental attitudes and assumptions of colonial religious conservatives of the eighteenth century.

One part of the attack was directed less against Whitefield and the other leaders than upon the lesser evangelists and the lay exhorters of the revival. The conservative Presbyterian ministers of the Middle Colonies, many of them educated in British universities, scorned the men trained at Tennent's "Log College." Though these young graduates had all undergone religious conversion and believed themselves led by God into the ministry, most of them had earlier followed other callings. If Gilbert Tennent could be persuaded, his opponents said, "to remit these strollers to their looms, their lasts, their packs, their grubbing hoes, from whence in his great zeal he took them to support his father's Log House College, we might soon hope to see a new face of affairs."[25] Charles Chauncy of Boston was even more vitriolic in his comments. These exhorters, he said, "are men of all occupations, who are vain enough to think themselves fit to be teachers of others; men who, though they have no learning and but small capacities, yet imagine they are able, and without study, too, to speak to the spiritual profit of such as are willing to hear them. Nay, there are among these exhorters, babes in age as well as understanding. They are chiefly, indeed, young persons, sometimes lads, or rather boys; nay, women and girls; yea, Negroes, have taken upon them to do the business of preachers."[26]

The attitude of the learned clergy on this matter seems on its face a blatant example of intellectual snobbery. These men, educated at Harvard or Yale or in the universities of the British Isles, seemed to arrogate to themselves the sole right of expounding God's Word to the masses of His children. Other men, equally or even more imbued with the Holy Spirit, were to keep silent, simply because they had been less exposed to formal schooling in their youth. Education, and sometimes the economic and social background which made that education possible, seemed to be substituted for spiritual insight and power as the prerequisites for the Christian ministry. There was in this attitude something of the intellectual Pharisaism which has appeared in many other cultured groups in history.

But the attitude of the educated clergy was not due entirely

[25] Quoted in Maxson, *Great Awakening in the Middle Colonies*, pp. 96–97.

[26] Chauncy, *Seasonable Thoughts*, p. 226.

to snobbery, especially among the Presbyterians and Congregationalists, who made the most frequent attacks on the unlearned revivalists. There was something fundamental in the insistence of these denominations on a high educational requirement for the ministry. As two modern scholars have recently pointed out, "interpretation of scripture was an abstruse art, to be learned with diligence, to be employed with caution, and to be regulated by the immutable laws of right reason and infallible logic."[27] The untrained exhorter, mistaking zeal and "sudden impulses" for true understanding, might quite unwittingly serve as the mouthpiece of Satan while professing to expound God's Holy Word. His false preaching would be no less dangerous because done with honest intent and with a firm trust in spiritual guidance. To insist, therefore, upon a learned ministry trained to the use of reason was not merely to "unionize" the pulpit for the benefit of its current incumbents but even more to protect the church from the fatal consequences of ministerial ignorance.

A somewhat different form of class consciousness is suggested by the charge that the revival was keeping men from their daily labor. Such statements, while not relatively numerous, come from all parts of the colonies. Characteristic of them all was the comment of Commissary Dawson of Virginia. Writing to the Bishop of London in 1750, he mentioned as one of his criticisms of the evangelist Samuel Davies, "his holding forth on working days to great numbers of poor people, who generally are his only followers. This certainly is inconsistent with the religion of labor," Dawson went on, "whereby they are obliged to maintain themselves and their families, and their neglect of this duty if not seasonably prevented may in process of time be sensibly felt by the government."[28]

The concern which these men felt for the neglected families

[27] Perry Miller and Thomas H. Johnson, eds., *The Puritans* (New York and Cincinnati: American Book Company, [*ca.* 1938]), p. 25.

[28] Perry, *Historical Collections*, I, 366.

of the "poor" or "vulgar" who attended these frequent meetings may have been based simply on religious or humanitarian grounds. But there are overtones in all such comments that hint of something else. It should be remembered that clergymen who suggested that the common people were neglecting the "religion of labor" in their concern for their immortal souls were themselves nearly always, socially at least, members of the upper class. Because of their education and their professional positions and regardless of the amount of their income, these wearers of the ministerial broadcloth were accepted on terms of equality by the wealthy and the aristocratic. Almost always they absorbed, at least to some degree, the point of view of the privileged class. It was right and necessary, they agreed, that the laboring classes should be faithful in church attendance and in the practice of all the Christian virtues. But the workers' station in society also required of them honest toil. They ought to remember God's judgment upon Adam, "In the sweat of thy face shalt thou eat bread," and not let a craze for attending religious meetings interfere with the long hours of good hard work that were the proper weekday occupation of the "multitude." For the common people to neglect the "religion of labor" was to forget their duty and dangerously to undermine the foundation of society. The ministerial rebukes were, in part at least, an expression of conservative class consciousness.

One of the most widespread criticisms of the revival was that of its emotionalism. Conservatives of all denominations united in denouncing "enthusiasm" in language which suffered few restraints. The very words "enthusiasm" and "enthusiast" became terms of reproach and suspicion in much the same way that "Communism" and "Communist" are regarded by most Americans today. When one minister might express his amazement "to see how fond the common people here are of novelties in religion, how easily they become a prey to seducers," another would express the same feeling by saying he was surprised "to observe how the vulgar everywhere are inclined to enthusiasm."[29] One writer called Whitefield a "rant" and "novice"; others referred to him as a "fanatic" or a "deceiver"; while still another, after first speaking of him as an "imposter" and as an "incendiary," later thought it enough to call him simply "that wild enthusiast."[30] According to the Philadelphia Presbyterian Synod, the enthusiasts preached "the terrors of the Law in such manner and dialect as has no precedent in the Word of God." They so worked "on the passions and affections of weak minds as to cause them to cry out in a hideous manner and fall down in convulsion-like fits, to the marring of the profiting both of themselves and others, who are so taken up in seeing and hearing these odd symptoms that they cannot attend to or hear what the preacher says."[31] When the revival storm struck a community there appeared to the conservative observer a veritable "tempest of enthusiasm," in which "the sea roared indeed and the waves rose so high that to face them was present shipwreck."[32]

[29] *Ibid.*, II, 208, V, 83.

[30] *South-Carolina Gazette*, August 23–30, 1742, No. 440; Perry, *Historical Collections*, II, 207, 209, 204–5; V, 84.

[31] Tracy, *Great Awakening*, pp. 71–72.

[32] Perry, *Historical Collections*, II, 204. A graphic, though hostile, description of such scenes comes from an Anglican minister of Massachusetts: "Their behavior is indeed as shocking, as uncommon; their groans, cries, screams, and agonies must affect the spectators were they never so obdurate, and draw tears even from the most resolute, whilst the ridiculous and frantic gestures of others cannot but excite both laughter and contempt, some leaping, some laughing, some singing, some clapping one another upon the back, etc. The tragic scene is performed by such as are entering into the pangs of the New Birth, the comic by those who are got through and those are so truly enthusiastic that they tell you they saw the joys of Heaven, can describe its situation, inhabitants, employments, and have seen their names entered into the Book of Life and can point out the writer, character, and pen." *Ibid.*, III, 343.

However effective this emotionalism might seem to others, to conservatives it was a dangerous innovation and no proper part of the Christian tradition as handed down from past generations. It was therefore suspect and rightly to be condemned. Sincere men of all denominations could agree with one Church of England minister who told his congregation: "Religion is not founded upon such sudden impulses and raving expressions, but upon faith and a sincere obedience."[33] Upon such grounds earnest conservatives, regardless of their differences on other points, could unite in denouncing the enthusiasts as "false prophets and pretended saints."[34]

In the last analysis, the revival seemed most dangerous because it was so upsetting to the peace and order of the churches. Wherever the evangelists went they stirred people out of their usual complacency, not only to a search for personal salvation, but also to a questioning of each other's sanctification and to a dissatisfaction with the spiritual food offered in their churches. There were conservative ministers of all denominations who would sincerely welcome a quickening of religion among their congregations if only it did not seem to bring with it greater evils than the apathy and listlessness it replaced. They were willing to admit, in many cases, that the awakening had been useful, but in some of its phases it was doing more harm than good by arousing unchristian animosities, by disturbing the orderly services of religion, and by undermining the discipline of the churches.

It is the very essence of the conservative attitude to wish to preserve in its fundamentals the *status quo*. In the religious field that meant, among other things, that the organization of the particular denomination to which such a conservative belonged ought to remain intact and its discipline in full force. But the

[33] *Ibid.*, III, 364.
[34] *Ibid.*, II, 449.

itinerants were not particularly interested in denominational organization. Whitefield, for example, although an Anglican, preached in churches of other denominations without hesitation and accepted in full brotherhood ministers who had never received episcopal ordination. To loyal Church of England men, this sort of thing was nothing less than treason against the Church. But others could object on even more serious grounds. In 1740 a pamphlet called *The Querists* appeared in Philadelphia attacking Whitefield on several counts. Among other things it charged him with displaying too tolerant a spirit; if he, an Anglican, was willing to join with Antinomians, Arminians, Calvinists, and Lutherans in religious work, why not — horror of horrors — even with the Papists at Rome?[35] To men bred in the traditions of Protestant denominational orthodoxy, whatever their particular formula for salvation, such heterodoxy was, in effect, a direct assault upon the Faith.

Quite apart from issues of denominational integrity, the revival seemed to many sincere churchmen to threaten the essentials of church unity and Christian discipline. When itinerant preachers, following Whitefield's example, "thrust themselves into towns and parishes" and publicly attacked the spiritual state of resident ministers, they were working "to the destruction of all peace and order." The people thereafter were "ready to despise their own ministers," and the pastors' usefulness seemed almost to have been destroyed.[36] The first consequence of such a state of affairs was a collapse of church discipline. Conservatives in any field of thought or action are almost always believers in discipline. They would agree with the Reverend Charles Chauncy when he pointed out that "*Discipline* is necessary in

[35] [Thomas Evans], *The Querists, or, An Extract of Sundry Passages Taken Out of Mr. Whitefield's Printed Sermons, Journals, and Letters* (Philadelphia, 1740), p. 24.

[36] From the Testimony of the Harvard Faculty against Whitefield, December 28, 1744. Tracy, *Great Awakening*, pp. 349–50.

all societies whatever; and where this is neglected, if there is the appearance of confusion, what is it more than may justly be expected?"[37] Now when the itinerants were undermining the loyalty of congregations to their own ministers, they were undermining discipline.

A second and still more deadly consequence of this assault upon the spiritual integrity of ministers and churches was the growth of separatism. When, as often happened, a minority of a particular Puritan congregation came under the influence of revivalistic ideas and were persuaded that the established minister of their church was not a true Christian and that their fellow members were equally unsaved, they were very likely to withdraw and form a church society of their own. An intense struggle then took place between the "Old Light" and the "New Light" churches of New England over control of the church property and over the taxation of the "New Light" members for support of the regularly established "Old Light" ministers. Sometimes a whole church, desiring to induct as minister a candidate whom the sister churches of neighboring communities considered too radical, defied its conservative critics and installed the minister anyway, thereby cutting itself off from the fellowship of the other congregations. Among the Presbyterians a somewhat similar controversy led to the withdrawal of the New Brunswick Presbytery from the Philadelphia Synod in 1741 and to the formation of the separate New York Synod a few years later. Some of the smaller denominations suffered also.

This was a distressing situation and one to be fought with Christian zeal. In this emergency the conservatives did what they could to check the forces of separation. In South Carolina, Commissary Alexander Garden, one of Whitefield's sharpest critics, summoned the evangelist to trial before an ecclesiastical

---

[37] Chauncy, *Seasonable Thoughts*, p. 423.

court, the only one of its kind ever held by an Anglican authority among the Continental colonies. Whitefield challenged Garden's jurisdiction and appealed to England. There, on technical
grounds, the appeal was dropped. The General Court of Virginia, controlled by conservatives, took over from the county
courts the licensing of dissenting preachers and tried, not too
successfully, to limit the number of evangelists and the places at
which they could hold forth. In Connecticut, where the "Old
Lights" held control of the government, James Davenport, the
most extreme of the itinerants, was brought before the assembly
in 1742 for his disturbance of the religious peace. After examining him the legislature concluded that he was insane and ordered
him sent back to his own parish on Long Island. The next year
they passed an act which withdrew much of the toleration that
had been permitted to nonconforming groups and individuals
since 1708. A number of the "New Lights" were fined and a
few imprisoned for failure to pay church rates for the benefit
of established ministers. Two Yale students were expelled by
the authorities of that orthodox and conservative institution for
having attended a Separatist church with their parents during
the vacation. The radicals in turn were aroused by this persecution; gradually their party increased in political strength, and
between 1770 and 1777, in spite of all the conservatives could
do, the "New Lights" finally gained control and passed legislation giving their churches a measure of real equality within the
colony.

Thus most of the efforts of conservatives to stem the tide of
separation failed in the end, even in those colonies where their
churches enjoyed the privilege of establishment. It could not
be expected that conservative leaders of less favored churches
or those in colonies where there was no establishment would be
any more successful. Every denomination felt, to a greater or
lesser degree, the disruptive influence of the revival upon its

discipline and its unity in spite of all efforts to hold the radicals in line and to punish those who defied the authority of the organization. Discipline and unity seemed lost forever.

To men who believed in these organizations and who held that it was the duty of all true Christians "to stand up for the *good old way*" as defined by their particular denominations, the consequences of the Great Awakening were sad indeed. Where once there had been brotherhood now there were animosities and bitterness; where once each church group and its members had stood as one in the face of all outside foes, they now fought as fiercely among themselves as if they were mortal enemies. The "divisions, separations, and confusions" which the revival inflicted on each denomination seemed to its conservative adherents a deep betrayal of the cause of Christ.

The Great Awakening has appeared to many historians, in retrospect, a great agency for good, kindling a new religious spirit in the lives of thousands and providing a unifying cultural force which transcended the narrow provincialism of colonial life. With the perspective of two centuries we can see, too, that the evangelical Protestantism which the revival fostered became in time a great creative and energizing power, responsible for much that has been most typical of later American society. But to many sincere Christians of the time these benefits were not so clear or were more than offset by the evils that seemed to accompany them.

To men living through a period of upheaval—which the Great Awakening certainly was—the social benefits that may ultimately emerge are at best problematical, while the immediate dangers and injuries are very real and often very personal. It is natural that men of a conservative temperament should see and emphasize those dangers and injuries and should minimize or entirely fail to foresee the gains which the upheaval may bring forth at the expense of established institutions. Later generations, on the contrary, tend to view such a period with a different perspective; to them the long-run benefits far outweigh the immediate costs. So it has been with the Great Awakening. We of the twentieth century can see that the revival stimulated a new and invigorating religious life and laid the foundation for the tremendous growth of evangelical Christianity which later played so important a part in the development of American culture. But we ought also to remember that the vision of that future was not revealed to the men of the eighteenth century and that to thousands of sincere Christians the Great Awakening seemed to menace much of what they held dear in the religious life of their times. Only by appreciating the attitude of these conservatives as well as that of the revivalists can we understand fully this significant episode in American religious history.

EDUCATION AND SOCIAL THEORY

"The relinquishment of old opinions," once declared a colonial minister, "or the adoption of new ones, without sufficient examination and evidence, are equally proofs of weak minds, and equally criminal."[1] Men of a conservative temperament, of all countries and ages, would be inclined to agree. New ideas and new attitudes may be very well in their place and may contribute to what the nineteenth century came to call "Progress." But new opinions when adopted must displace old ones, and the true conservative is reluctant to make a change in a hurry or until he is thoroughly convinced of its necessity. He is skeptical of new ideas and unwilling to accept them, as the clergyman put it, "without a thorough conviction of their being well founded."

Conservative-minded men of the eighteenth century, in common with all others of their type, took this attitude toward the thought currents and the social theories of their day. Whatever field of thought or action might be concerned — whether ideas were in the realm of intellectual things, or involved issues of social relationships, or concerned even such a trivial matter as the wearing of a wig — the colonial conservative revealed himself by clinging tenaciously to the old, the tried, and the accustomed, and by looking with suspicion on that which was novel and unfamiliar.

In no field of human affairs was the essential conservatism of the controlling groups in the colonies more apparent than in

[1] Boucher, *American Revolution*, p. 63.

their handling of the problems of education. Limitations of space do not permit us to consider here the elementary and secondary schooling of the colonial period in full detail. That is far too large a topic for the present discussion. In relation to our general theme the chief point that comes out from a study of the schools is that neither in basic philosophy, method, nor content did the American educational system make any effective advances during the hundred years before the Revolution. American education was essentially conservative.

The Massachusetts school laws of 1642 and 1647 suggested somewhat vaguely the principle of universal compulsory education of an elementary nature and specified that the initial responsibility for providing education rested with the local community. These are among the basic principles of the present-day public-school system of almost all the United States. The Massachusetts laws were closely followed by similar legislation in Connecticut, and some steps were taken in the same direction in other colonies in the seventeenth century. Yet not even in their New England home were these principles adequately carried out during the entire colonial period. The third fundamental concept of our present system of public education—that schooling ought to be free so far as the individual child is concerned—did not make an effective appearance until after the Revolution. While a few free schools existed for the children of the poor, these were regarded as strictly charity foundations. Here and there a school was tax-supported or rested on an endowment, but these were exceptions to the common rule that education was a commodity to be paid for like any other.

In method and content the schools made little progress in the eighteenth century. Learning continued to be largely a matter of rote with a plentiful application of corporal punishment. The elementary schools dealt with the "Three R's" and the elements of religion, and little else. The secondary "grammar" schools prepared for college by pounding away at the classics, particularly Latin. Except for a little surveying, navigation, or commercial arithmetic offered here and there as a sop to those of a more practical turn of mind, secondary education had little relation to the special conditions of American society. For the vast majority of colonial youth it offered no training that would prepare them for life. Until practically the end of the period only a few leaders of thought and action like Benjamin Franklin ventured to suggest any fundamental changes in the pattern or the content of formal education up to the college level. Training for the crafts, and to a large extent for the professions of medicine and law as well, was conducted through apprenticeship and not through the organized school system. Men generally accepted for their children or their neighbors' children just the same sort of schooling they had received themselves.

The more conservative among them even objected to any change in the textbooks used for their children's schooling. The Virginia planter Robert Carter's attitude was characteristic when he was giving directions for his sons' education in England. "I could wish," he wrote in 1724, "Mr. Low [the schoolmaster] had kept in the old way of teaching the Latin tongue and had made my boys perfect in their understand of Lily's *Grammar* and of the old schoolbooks that we and our forefathers learned." One book in particular, first published in English over fifty years before, was in Carter's memory so splendid a work that he ordered his son removed from the school he was attending if the master did not forthwith adopt it as a text.[2] Fashions in textbooks change much more rapidly now than they did two centuries ago, and parents have become somewhat hardened to the situation, but there may be some schoolteachers

[2] Wright, *The First Gentlemen of Virginia*, pp. 251–52, quoting from *Virginia Magazine of History and Biography*, XXXI (January 1923), 39–40 n.

or administrators even today who have met parents as meddle-some and as conservative as Robert Carter.

In their influence upon the social order schools can be among the most important of all institutions. Recognizing this fact, conservatives have often tried to ensure that their children would be exposed in school only to the "right" sort of ideas and taught only by the "right" sort of people. Within the past quarter-century we have seen several examples of such an attitude. Soon after the First World War there was a wave of criticism of textbooks of American history on the score that they were "unpatriotically" presenting the British and Tory side of the Revolution and so corrupting the pupil's patriotism. The works of eminent historians who had tried to be fair and impartial were therefore banned with little or no inquiry into the essential accuracy of their contents. A few years later there was a movement in some sections to require a special oath of loyalty from all teachers. Ardent conservatives regarded educators as a special class of citizens whose patriotism must be as free from suspicion as the virtue of Caesar's wife. In several communities, therefore, teachers in private as well as public schools, from the kindergarten to the graduate school, were subjected to a special oath of loyalty not required of the ordinary member of society.

This attitude toward schools and teachers is by no means new. It is likely to appear whenever the body politic is undergoing a period of special stress. Even the proposal for a teachers' oath is no invention of the twentieth century. In the period just before the American Revolution it was advanced by that stalwart conservative, Jonathan Boucher. Some of the governmental leaders of Maryland asked him to prepare a sermon on education for a meeting in 1773 that was to consider the consolidation of three free schools. The most interesting passage in this address had to do with the qualifications of the master of the proposed school. According to Boucher, he must have "zeal for the Christian religion; diligence in his calling; affection to the present government; and conformity to the doctrine and discipline of the Church of England." Then, following the example of the Society for Promoting Charity Schools in Ireland, he should be required to subscribe a solemn declaration that:

He does heartily acknowledge His Majesty King George to be the only rightful and lawful king of these realms; and will, to the utmost of his power, educate the children committed to his charge in a true sense of their duty to him as such;

That he will not, by any words or actions, do anything whereby to lessen their esteem of, or their obedience to, the present Government;

That, upon all public days, when the children of this school may be likely to bear a part in any tumults or riots (which are an affront to Government, and so great a scandal, as well as prejudice, to these realms) he will do his best to keep them in and restrain such licentiousness;

And likewise, if there be any catechisms or institutions which teach or encourage any exceptionable political or party principles, such as are incompatible with the law and the Constitution of this country, he will immediately throw them aside as pernicious to the original design of this pious nursery.[3]

Change the object of loyalty from British King and Government to American Constitution, modernize the phraseology and literary style, and you will have here a declaration that would suit admirably those citizens who have advocated teachers' oaths in the twentieth-century United States. Conservatives are seldom innovators.

The colonial colleges, designed to provide a liberal education to fit young men "for public employment both in church and civil state," offer another instructive example of the conservative influence in early American education. Let us consider the curriculum. In these days when the frequent revision of the requirements for a degree is one of the leading indoor sports of

[3] Boucher, *American Revolution*, pp. 195–96.

college faculties; when liberal-arts programs vary as widely as those of St. John's College and Bennington; when our leading colleges accept for the Bachelor of Arts degree courses in such relatively newfangled subjects as Commercial Banking, International Relations, and the American Family; when the graduate and professional schools of time-honored universities offer serious training in such diverse matters as the Malayan Language, Modern Office Appliances, and Tap Dancing; when, in short, higher education for Americans appears to have lost all semblance of common plan or common purpose, then the traditionalism, the uniformity, and the essential conservatism of the curriculum of the colonial colleges becomes especially striking.

The nine colleges offering the bachelor's degree during the colonial period were: Harvard, William and Mary, Yale, the College of New Jersey (now Princeton), the College of Philadelphia (now the University of Pennsylvania), King's (now Columbia), Rhode Island (now Brown), Queen's (now Rutgers), and Dartmouth.

From the founding of Harvard in 1636 to the chartering of Dartmouth in 1769, the curriculum of the colonial colleges remained unchanged in all important respects and was essentially the same in all nine institutions.[4] It was derived from the course of study in the universities of the British Isles and was based squarely upon the system of education in all the great universities of medieval Europe. With minor variations here and there

[4] Among college histories the following provide the most helpful discussions of the curriculum before the Revolution: Samuel E. Morison, *The Founding of Harvard College* (Cambridge: Harvard University Press, 1935); Samuel E. Morison, *Three Centuries of Harvard, 1636–1936* (Cambridge: Harvard University Press, 1936); Edward P. Cheyney, *History of the University of Pennsylvania, 1740–1940* (Philadelphia: University of Pennsylvania Press, 1940); and Thomas J. Wertenbaker, *Princeton, 1746–1896* (Princeton: Princeton University Press, 1946).

and with slightly differing emphasis between the seventeenth and the eighteenth centuries it can be described as follows: Students were examined at admission upon their command of Latin and their ability to read and conjugate simple Greek. In their first two years they usually continued their study of the classical authors but devoted most of their time to the famous medieval *trivium:* grammar (that is, Latin grammar), rhetoric, and logic. In the last two years the curriculum everywhere included mathematics and the three philosophies: mental philosophy, or metaphysics; moral philosophy, or ethics; and natural philosophy. This last we would today list under the heading of "science." It consisted mostly of physics, with some elements of astronomy, and occasionally a little chemistry thrown in. Sometimes students in their senior year also studied theology, not, however, in an advanced or technical form as training for the ministry, but on a broad basis, involving only such aspects of the subject as any intelligent, well-educated Christian might be expected to understand. With the advance of experimental science in the eighteenth century the colleges gave somewhat more attention to natural philosophy, and there is some evidence that what we would call psychology and political science won increased treatment under the headings of mental and moral philosophy. But with these exceptions the curriculum of the American colleges remained practically unchanged until after the Revolution. Even at the one nonsectarian college, Philadelphia (now the University of Pennsylvania), where the influence of Benjamin Franklin was strong, plans to apply more "modern" educational theories made really very little headway during this period against the generally prevailing ideas of what a university education ought to include. The son of a New England Puritan at Harvard or Yale, of a Virginia planter at William and Mary, of a Rhode Island merchant at what is now Brown University, or even an Indian youth at Dartmouth were all subjected to the common principle that to "educate" a man you should drill him in Latin, logic, and metaphysics. The old education was the sound education.

In another respect, too, the colleges, without exception, clung tenaciously to the pattern of the past. An important part of the students' work during the final two years was the so-called disputations. Conducted regularly, normally once a week, and under the watchful eye of the most distinguished member of the faculty, who was usually the president himself, these exercises consisted of the formal defense of some philosophical proposition. The students were taught to present their cases and to attack each other's arguments according to the most rigid rules of logic. The purpose was, above all else, to develop the capacity to think and reason clearly.

At the commencement exercises the students had printed and distributed a broadside sheet containing, in Latin, some seventy-five or a hundred of these propositions, or theses, which the graduating seniors were prepared to defend publicly upon demand. Usually one or two of these were called for, possibly by prearrangement, and the young candidates for the bachelor's degree received the opportunity to show how well they had learned not only the subject under consideration but the art of logical demonstration of a proposition. Many of these broadsides still exist. Dr. James J. Walsh has made a study of them in his book *Education of the Founding Fathers of the Republic.*[5] In his analysis Dr. Walsh emphasizes two points which are of importance to this discussion of conservatism. In the first place, this whole system of disputation is a direct inheritance from the medieval universities. These regular exercises, culminating in a public exhibition when the students were about to receive their degrees, were almost exact replicas of the exercises that had been carried on in every great European university for over five hun-

[5] New York: Fordham University Press, 1935.

dred years. By publishing these commencement theses, these upstart colonial colleges let the world know that they were no innovators; they were following, on the contrary, the traditions and the practices of centuries of European educators.

In the second place, a substantial proportion of these theses, the concepts they illustrated, and the very phrases they used are the direct embodiment of medieval Scholastic philosophy. Scholasticism, the great intellectual edifice built up in the Middle Ages and associated with the names of such great Schoolmen and thinkers as Duns Scotus, St. Anselm, and St. Thomas Aquinas, by no means died out with the Renaissance. It persisted in the great European universities and was brought over by Oxford and Cambridge graduates to the English colonies. Scholastic philosophy did not monopolize the intellectual life of Harvard or King's College or Princeton any more than it did that of Oxford and Cambridge or the Scottish universities in the seventeenth and eighteenth centuries, and many propositions unknown to the medieval Schoolmen appeared on the American commencement thesis papers; nevertheless, it is clear that Scholasticism and the Scholastic method remained as a continuing and very living force in the educational system of the American colonial colleges. The old ideas had proved serviceable for a long time and they were not to be discarded lightly.

I have emphasized the general uniformity of the education systems in all nine of the colonial colleges. Perhaps it would be correct to suggest, however, that the similarity among them seems to us today to be more complete than it did to men of the eighteenth century. One important reason for the founding of Yale in 1701, for example, was the belief, widely held among the most orthodox Puritans, that Harvard had become too radical. This feeling was shared not only by ministers of ultraconservative Connecticut, but also by many in Massachusetts, including those stanch gentlemen of the old school, Increase and

Cotton Mather. The founders of the new Collegiate School, as it was first called, received encouragement and help in their new venture from the Mathers and other like-minded Bostonians. Princeton, on the other hand, was founded by supporters of the Great Awakening, and even so thoroughly a Calvinist institution seemed, for a time at least, to be an object of suspicion to "Old Light" clergymen and their parishioners. As for the College of Philadelphia, it provided the one real innovation in that, alone of all the colonial colleges, it had no denominational origin, but was established on a strictly nonsectarian basis. In this respect rather than in its curriculum, the Philadelphia college pointed the way to the future. Thus the colleges seemed to their contemporaries to be rather more varied in character than we might readily admit.

The fact that the so-called dissenting sects controlled higher education everywhere in the North until the middle of the eighteenth century was a source of distress to Anglicans, who looked upon the colleges, particularly Harvard and Yale in New England, as dangerously republican in tendency and influence. Lewis Morris, Anglican, landed proprietor of New York and New Jersey, and governor of the latter colony, was so concerned over the situation that he stipulated in his will that his son Gouverneur should not be educated in Connecticut. He feared, as he stated in his last testament, that at Yale the boy would "imbibe in his youth that low craft and cunning so incident to the people of that colony, which is so interwoven in their constitutions that all their art cannot disguise it from the world, though many of them under the sanctified garb of Religion, have endeavored to impose themselves on the world for honest men."[6] For the son of one habituated to leadership among

---

[6] Mark, *Agrarian Conflicts*, p. 99, quoting from *Abstract of Wills* . . . . *City of New York, 1665–1800* (Collections of the New-York Historical Society, New York, 1898), VI, 174.

the gentry of New York and New Jersey, as Morris was, Connecticut could offer only a dangerously leveling and hypocritical sort of education.

It was in part because of this dislike of New England educational facilities that residents of New York undertook to found King's College, now Columbia University. They inoculated the new institution against the virus of Puritanism by naming as its first president the Reverend Samuel Johnson, former tutor at Yale and former minister of a Congregational church, who had been converted to Anglicanism, taken Holy Orders, and for thirty-one years had been rector of the pioneer Anglican church in Connecticut at Stratford. A safe, conservative, but distinguished leadership was what Johnson, above all others, could be expected to supply. Some years later, just before the beginning of the Revolution, the backers of the college desired to bolster its position still further by securing a royal charter. In transmitting to Governor Tryon the draft of such a charter, Cadwallader Colden called attention to the dissenters' near-monopoly of higher education in the colonies. It seemed to him "highly requisite that a seminary on the principles of the Church of England be distinguished in America by particular privileges, not only on account of religion, but of good policy, to prevent the farther growth of republican principles, which already too much prevail in the colonies." [7] Here was another illustration of the widely held theory that an educational institution ought to exert primarily a conservative influence on the community.

Education, as most of us believe, is one of the foundations of society. It can be an instrument of progress, preparing each new generation for its own day, helping young men and women to deal intelligently and usefully with the ever-changing problems they will face, both as individuals and as members of a complex society. Or education can be essentially a conservative force,

[7] *Colden Letter Books*, II, 355; *N.Y. Col. Docs.*, VIII, 486.

emphasizing that which lies in the past and has become a part of man's heritage, and equipping young people with the same tools their fathers used to construct the society of their time. Ideally, education should be both things. It should conserve for each generation all the best that has been said and done through the long years of civilization, and at the same time open up so far as possible the vistas of the future and show to young men and women how, by using the great faculties of the human mind, they can hope to march down the avenue of life with confidence and strength.

As I have tried to show in this brief analysis, education, as organized in the colonial period, emphasized almost wholly its conservative function. In a changing world and in a new environment it made no significant changes to meet new needs. In content and in substance it clung to the patterns made familiar by five centuries of English and continental tradition. It took pride in its identity with the educational system of the Old World and made few if any concessions to the new conditions. At the college level it did, however, teach men to think, and by that one fact it enabled the sons of the last colonial generation to grow into the strong leaders of a new nation and to build wisely the foundations of a new and an American society.

We must turn now to consideration of the social setting of this educational system and to the attitude of the colonial conservative to the changes in the life and customs which inevitably took place. For in every phase of human affairs the passage of time as well as the new environment brought changes. Society and social practices never remain the same for very long.

In his attitude toward innovations in social customs the colonial conservative ran true to the pattern of his individual or group antecedents and beliefs. Those colonists whose background and upbringing included toleration of particular forms of behavior felt no concern when these first appeared in America. Other men, whose ancestors had looked on such practices as harmful or improper, tended to object strenuously to their introduction to the colonies and to do everything possible to prevent their spread. The theater offers a good example of such an innovation. To the more worldly colonists, especially in the Middle and Southern provinces, the play was essentially a source of enjoyment and a form of culture, not inherently harmful, even though some of them would admit that the English stage of the Restoration Era left something to be desired in the decency of its offerings and in the morals of its performers. The first theater in America was opened at Williamsburg, Virginia, in 1716, and plays were fairly common in the more southerly colonies after the middle of the eighteenth century. But the Puritans of New England and the Quakers and Presbyterians of Pennsylvania had inherited a different tradition. Their forefathers had been revolted by the licentiousness of the English stage and had transmitted to their descendants a belief that actors and their performances were not only to be shunned by the godly but to be fought against as a matter of public duty by every right-minded citizen.

When, about the middle of the century, the Hallam troupe, later known as the American Company of Comedians, made their appearance in the colonies, they encountered a mixed reception. Because of the cosmopolitan character of Philadelphia and its position as the largest city in the colonies, the playhouse there proved to be one of the most profitable places on the troupe's itinerary. But many worthy burghers were shocked at the actors' popularity in the Quaker capital, and a sharp newspaper controversy took place there as late as the very eve of the Revolution. One spokesman for the conservatives emphasized the sorrow of "many sober inhabitants of different denominations" when they heard of the return, after a tour, "of those strolling comedians who are traveling through America propagating vice and immorality." He appealed to the magistrates to run them out of town on the strength of old English statutes against strolling players, vagabonds, and sturdy beggars. The playhouse, he said, collected crowds, obstructed traffic, and disturbed the neighborhood. But worst of all, the indignant citizen wrote, "it is notorious that so far from virtue's being recommended [in the theater] to the imitation of the people, ... vice and immorality are there exhibited in such pleasing colors as to induce many giddy and unwary youth to realize and reduce to practice what they see displayed there under fictitious characters." The playhouse "without exaggeration may be called the school of vice and debauchery."[8] Others took up the cudgels in the papers, some to defend and some to attack the stage play and the actors.[9] In the end the defenders of civic virtue were defeated; whether for good or for ill, the theater as an institution had come to America to stay.

Few of the wealthier colonists who have left records of their attitude showed any conscious conservatism in the matter of fashions in dress. Most were eager to hear of changes in London styles and to order clothing in the very latest fashion. Only the distance from the British metropolis and the slowness and difficulty of transportation kept them from obeying at once, as far as their finances would permit, the latest dictates of the *beau monde*. But when a new style struck at a deep-seated tradition or was associated in any way with a public issue, there were always some stanch supporters of the older practice who refused to surrender to fashion. A case in point is the tenacity with which the Quakers clung to their habitual garb, even though the wealthy among them had their clothes made of the finest materials. Again, some of the descendants of the Puritan

[8] *Dunlap's Pennsylvania Packet, or, the General Advertiser*, November 8, 1773, No. 107.

[9] *Ibid.*, November 15 and 29, 1773, Nos. 108 and 110.

"Roundheads" objected strenuously to the appearance of periwigs in Boston at the end of the seventeenth century. Staid old
Judge Samuel Sewall was just such a gentleman of the old
school, as his diary repeatedly emphasizes. On one occasion he
expressed his surprise and distress at hearing no less a person
than Cotton Mather indirectly approve the new fashion. "I expected not to hear a vindication of periwigs in Boston pulpit by
Mr. Mather," he wrote sadly in 1691. "The Lord give me a
good heart and help me to know, and not only to know, but
also to do, His will; that my heart and head may be His."[10] A
decade later he recorded his attendance at a church other than
his own, partly because the minister who was to preach in his
regular church had taken to wearing a wig. To this entry Sewall
added piously, "He that contemns the Law of Nature is not fit
to be a publisher of the Law of Grace."[11] When Ezekiel Cheever,
New England's grand old schoolmaster, died in 1708, full of
years and service, Sewall recorded the event in his diary and
added a biographical note describing Cheever's long life of usefulness and piety. The note ends with these words of eulogy:
"So that he has labored in the calling skillfully, diligently, constantly, religiously, seventy years. A rare instance of piety,
health, strength, serviceableness. The welfare of the province
was much upon his spirit. He abominated periwigs."[12] It is
doubtful if Sewall thought of the final sentence as in any way
an anticlimax.

The social theory upon which the colonial conservatives expressed themselves most fully and which has the deepest significance for an understanding of the period was that involving the
class structure of society. Many of us are inclined, perhaps, to
think of America through all its history as a land where class

[10] Sewall, *Diary*, I, 342.
[11] *Ibid.*, II, 48–49.
[12] *Ibid.*, II, 231.

distinctions have been of no great importance and where a man may rise as high as his own abilities and opportunities permit. In a relative sense there is much truth in such a picture and it has long been a part of the "American dream" and the "American tradition." Certainly if we compare the fluidity of society here with that of even the least solidified social systems of the Old World, the contrast is remarkable. But in an absolute sense America has never been as completely free from social stratification as superficial observers would have one believe.

In the English society from which most of the colonists had come there were certain distinct gradations, starting at the top with the aristocracy, which would include the members of the peerage and the country gentry, then running down through the rest of the gentleman class to the merchants, yeomen, tenant farmers, artisans, and agricultural laborers. In all classes it was possible for a son to rise to a higher level than his father had reached, or to drop a rank or two, so that from generation to generation there was considerable movement of individual families among the groups. At any given moment, however, the lines were rather sharply drawn; a man belonged to a particular class and was accorded the recognition and the privileges associated with his status. Furthermore, in eighteenth-century England the word "gentleman" had a very specific connotation. It meant a man well-born, one of a good family. A gentleman did not demean himself by manual labor or even by being, as we should say, "in business." The term did not yet have its derived meaning of "a man of gentle or refined manners." Certain manners were desirable in a gentleman but their possession or the lack of them had little to do with the fundamental tests of membership in the class of gentlemen.

Conditions in the colonies created certain differences in the social system from the start, though the concept of the gentleman was an essential element in the prevailing social theory. There was, of course, no separate class of nobility in the colonies, so that, with the exception of the governor, who took precedence as direct representative of the king or proprietor, the "gentlemen" stood at the top of the social hierarchy. The class of gentlemen, however, was somewhat more inclusive in America than in England. The great planters and the wealthy merchants, even though they all engaged in trade, called themselves "gentlemen" and were so regarded by most of their American contemporaries. Most of the clergy and the leading lawyers stood socially on a par with them, so that the term came to include practically all members of the upper, privileged groups. Below them were a large class of small landowners, some tenant farmers, and an increasing number of shopkeepers, artisans, and day laborers in the towns. Lower still were the indentured servants and the slaves. Members of the privileged upper class looked with complacency on the system. They accepted as inherent in mankind the inequality that made possible the concept of a gentleman. It was right that certain men should lead and others follow; and leadership carried with it the right to deference and social standing.[13]

The dominating position which the gentry occupied in the governmental and economic life was paralleled in the social

[13] On the doctrine of social inequality and the practice of social stratification, see especially Ebenezer Pemberton, *The Divine Original and Dignity of Government Asserted* (Boston, 1710), pp. 15–16; Miller and Johnson, *The Puritans*, pp. 16–19; *Colden Letter Books*, I, 231; II, 68–71; Mark, *Agrarian Conflicts*, pp. 55–56; Lincoln, *Revolutionary Movement in Pennsylvania*, pp. 85–86; William A. Schaper, "Sectionalism and Representation in South Carolina, a Sociological Study," *Annual Report* of the American Historical Association for 1900, I, pp. 273–74. The best discussion of the theory of the gentleman as exemplified in colonial America is in Wright, *First Gentlemen of Virginia*, particularly chap. i.

realm. The great planters of the South not only constituted a political oligarchy; they formed a social aristocracy as well, with all the pride and haughtiness that often goes with the attitude of a privileged group. In the eighteenth century a democratizing tendency in social relationships was already at work in some parts of the North and on the colonial frontiers generally, but it met only resistance in the tidewater regions of the South and from most of the gentry everywhere. The planter aristocrats, especially, seemed to consider themselves a race of superior beings.

When Philip Fithian went from his home in New Jersey to Virginia in 1774 to become a tutor in the home of Robert Carter, he was struck at once by the social attitude of his new employer and his friends. In New Jersey a certain degree of equality had prevailed. "Gentlemen in the first rank of dignity and quality," he wrote, " . . . . associate freely and commonly with farmers and mechanics, though they be poor and industrious." Ingenuity and industry were what really counted. "But you will find the tables turned the minute you enter [Virginia]. The very slaves in some families here could not be bought under £30,000 Such amazing property . . . . blows up the owners to an imagination which is visible in all" so that they seemed exalted above all other men in worth and precedency."[14]

The first Robert Carter, the grandfather of Fithian's employer, was probably the prime example of his class. The son of a seventeenth-century councilor, he was connected in varying degrees with a large proportion of the leading families of Virginia. As a young man he sat in the House of Burgesses, became its speaker, and then for thirty-two years was a member of the council. He served for over a year as president of Virginia after the death of Lieutenant Governor Drysdale in 1726. For a long period the agent of Lord Fairfax, proprietor of the Northern

[14] Farish, *Journal and Letters of Fithian*, pp. 210–11.

Neck, he used this position and his membership in the council to add enormously to his landholdings. When he died he was the owner of some one hundred thousand acres, the greatest landowner of his time in Virginia. This local pre-eminence strengthened what was by nature a proud and overbearing disposition and "King" Carter, as he was aptly called, became famous for his lordly airs, even in a circle noted for its self-esteem. Governor Francis Nicholson, who on occasion could match arrogance and temper with any man, wrote feelingly of Carter's "extraordinary pride and ambition, his using several people haughtily, sometimes making the justices of the peace of the county wait two or three hours before they can speak to him. . . . . To people that will flatter, cajole, and as it were adore him, he is familiar enough, but others he uses with all the haughtiness and insolence possible."[15] Carter's English background is uncertain. At most, his father, the founder of the Virginia line, belonged to a moderately wealthy family of the country gentry, but no noble lord of an ancient creation could have surpassed the class-conscious arrogance that Carter showed as a result of the position in provincial society his wealth and offices brought him.

Scornful attitudes were not reserved for the very bottom class of society alone. The aristocrats felt justified at times in using derogatory words even about the lesser planters. Soon after Bacon's Rebellion, inhabitants of Charles City County brought charges of corruption and oppression against Colonel Edward Hill, a large landowner and later a councilor. Realizing that his case was to be heard before a group of his fellow aristocrats, Hill had the tactical good sense to open his defense by disparaging his opponents. It was a hard thing, he said, "to be charged with several crimes and misdemeanors and clamored against by a route of people, how base, malicious, envious, and

[15] Quoted in [Harrison], *Virginia Land Grants*, p. 158.

ignorant soever," but history, even Virginia history, was full of just such cases of "brave, wise, just, and innocent good men that have fallen under the lash of that hydra the vulgar." Hill's tactics were sound. It is safe to say that even before he reached his detailed reply to the charges against him his aristocratic judges had been won to sympathy with his position. In the end he was completely exonerated.[16]

In their personal attitude toward the lower class the colonial aristocrats varied. Some might be haughty and overbearing under all circumstances, but probably few would express such lofty scorn for the more servile groups as did Jonathan Boucher. It was very likely after some especially exasperating experience, however, that he exclaimed: "If there be any particular class of mankind that are particularly unworthy and unamiable in my eyes, they are hackney-coachmen and postilions, gentlemen's footmen, and chambermaids at inns."[17]

At the same time, many of the gentry were kindly and generous in their dealings with the lesser folk. In his "History of the Dividing Line," for example, William Byrd II gives very clearly the impression that there was a good deal of friendly feeling between the boundary commissioners, on the one hand, all of whom were magnates of Virginia or North Carolina, and the men who did the rough work of the expedition, on the other. Although in his secret account he has some pretty caustic things to say about other commissioners, he spares no pains to praise the courage and the cheerfulness with which the rank and file faced the dangers and the hardships of the trip. A common experience produced a bond of comradeship which transcended the ordinary lines of class distinction.

Yet in the same work Byrd shows a different side. Again and

[16] "Defense of Col. Edward Hill," *Virginia Magazine*, III (January 1896), 239–52, 341–49; IV (July 1896), 1–15; especially III, 239.
[17] Boucher, *Reminiscences*, p. 173.

again he refers in contemptuous if semihumorous terms to the loutish inhabitants of the North Carolina back country. Without question most of his scorn was justified; the poor whites of that region were lazy, ignorant, and irreligious. But it is doubtful whether Byrd objected to the "drones" and "Hottentots" of his sister colony more because of these qualities than because of their disrespect for authority. "They are rarely guilty of flattering or making any court to their governors," he wrote, "but treat them with all the excesses of freedom and familiarity. They are of opinion their rulers would be apt to grow insolent if they grew rich, and for that reason take care to keep them poorer, and more dependent, if possible, than the saints in New England used to do their governors."[18] Perhaps Byrd wrote more truly than he knew. Many of these North Carolina border settlers had come originally from Virginia, where they had had a chance to observe the haughty airs put on by some of the planter aristocrats as their wealth increased. If in a new environment these plebeians were unwilling that their "rulers" become equally as "insolent" as many of the great men of Virginia undoubtedly were, their attitude is understandable. It is understandable, that is, to twentieth-century Americans, conditioned as we have been by the long growth of a democratic tradition. But to an eighteenth-century patrician, schooled in the aristocratic tradition of the country gentleman, such "leveling" principles as these people upheld were signs of a diseased condition of society, as distressing as the squalor and godlessness in which such frontiersmen lived.

The lower classes had their place in the scheme of things—no doubt of that. But it was clear to the gentlemen that these folk should keep that place and not trespass upon the position re-

[18] John S. Bassett, ed., *The Writings of "Colonel William Byrd of Westover in Virginia Esqr."* (New York: Doubleday, Page and Company, 1901), pp. 80–81. See also especially pp. 56, 58, 61, 75–76, 240–41.

served for their betters. The gentry were entitled to certain privileges which the common people might not share. There was the case, often cited, in 1674, of a certain tailor in Virginia who arranged a race between his mare and a horse belonging to one of the gentry. There was a handsome prize for the winner and presumably considerable betting took place among the spectators. But the court fined the tailor one hundred pounds of tobacco because, in the words of the record, it was "contrary to law for a laborer to make a race, [that] being a sport only for gentlemen." As for the gentleman in the case, the modern reader has a feeling of sardonic pleasure when he notes further in the record that the rich planter was sentenced to an hour in the stocks because he had arranged privately to throw the race to the tailor's mare.[19] Perhaps those who today are trying to stop professional gamblers from tampering with athletic contests might like to know about this precedent.

In matters of social intercourse the eighteenth-century code fixed a sharp line between the classes, not to be crossed from either side. In his "Journey to the Mines" Byrd tells the "tragical story" of a planter's daughter who married her uncle's overseer. Apparently the man was less to be condemned for his "impudence" than the girl for perpetrating "so senseless a prank," which was altogether defenseless in Byrd's eyes. "Had she run away with a gentleman or a pretty fellow," he pointed out, "there might have been some excuse for her, though he were of inferior fortune; but to stoop to a dirty plebeian, without any kind of merit, is the lowest prostitution."[20]

In nearly all the colonies the social division between the classes was clearly marked, but for those who knew and kept their place a gentleman might even feel considerable approval. Samuel Sewall mentions with some surprise but with apparent

[19] *William and Mary Quarterly*, 1st Series, III (October 1894), 136–37.
[20] Bassett, *Writings of William Byrd*, p. 338.

satisfaction a curious accident that occurred in a Boston church. A meeting of the membership was scheduled and in announcing it the minister, by a slip of the tongue, called for the attendance of the "gentlemen of the church and congregation." When the meeting took place only a few men were there. It developed that several members, recognizing that they were not "gentlemen" in the then accepted sense, held that they had not been summoned.[21] One may believe that the minister's embarrassment was considerable. He had violated the accepted social usage by employing the word "gentlemen" to refer to all male members of his congregation regardless of their social status. But the significant aspect of the incident is that there was evidently a good understanding in the community regarding who constituted the gentlemen, and that those who did not belong socially had voluntarily stayed away from the meeting. That, thought the members of the "better" class, was just as it should be.

When the lower classes began to forget their place, when the "vulgar" began to assume privileges that were not rightly theirs, when the "leveling" spirit of the frontier began to affect the social as well as the political behavior of the masses everywhere, then the gentry became disturbed. Throughout the criticism of the Great Awakening there runs a note of alarm at the social implications of the religious revival. Again and again in the course of their attacks, conservatives referred to the reception of the itinerant preachers by the "common people," the "giddy, ignorant people," and the "admiring vulgar," as if to imply that part of the evil done was the stirring up of the masses and the disturbance of the social order which inevitably followed. The bitter charge that "men, women, children, servants, and Negroes" were becoming lay exhorters and the contemptuous suggestion that Tennent send his "Log College" graduates back "to their looms, their lasts, their packs, their grubbing hoes"

[21] Sewall, *Diary*, II, 195–96.

were evidence not only of a desire to uphold the intellectual standards of the preaching ministry, but also of a disturbed class feeling on the part of the conservatives.[22] Men from the lower ranks of society had no right to leadership in the community, whether in the religious field or in any other.

When the period of agitation began which culminated in the Revolution the conflict between the social classes came out into the open. Leadership in the opposition to British legislation was at first in the hands of those who had always controlled public affairs. Unquestionably the burden of the stamp duties fell most heavily on the shoulders of the merchants, the lawyers, the men of property and education generally. But almost from the start the lower classes joined in the agitation. Very few members of the local organizations known as the "Sons of Liberty" were members of the colonial aristocracy. As early as 1765 it began to dawn on some of the upper rank that men of a social level that had never been deemed worthy of leadership were taking a prominent part in public affairs. Although few colonists of any class approved the legislative measures adopted by Great Britain, a substantial number came to feel that these represented far less of a menace than did the emergence of the lower orders. People "of the better sort" began to be "sensible of the great want of a reform," as the sister of a royal customs officer in Boston wrote in 1769, and to recognize that "the tyranny of the multitude is the most arbitrary and oppressive."[23]

As time wore on and the controversy intensified, the social danger became more apparent to men of the upper class. Many who had supported the earlier opposition to British policy now drew back, "more from interest than principle," the same lady

---

[22] See above, pp. 79–80.
[23] *Letters of a Loyalist Lady, Being the Letters of Ann Hulton Sister of Henry Hulton, Commissioner of Customs at Boston, 1767–1776* (Cambridge: Harvard University Press, 1927), p. 18.

said in the summer before the war. "The people of property, of best sense and characters," were recognizing that their security was being threatened by the "tyranny" of the new leaders and that the "authority of Parliament" was the lesser of the two evils.[24] A South Carolina clergyman, more outspoken than most, declared from the pulpit that "mechanics and country clowns had no right to dispute about politics, or what kings, lords, and commons had done." He was dismissed from his congregation for his stand and the patriotic Newport (Rhode Island) *Mercury* declared that "all such divines should be taught that mechanics and country clowns (infamously so-called) are the real and absolute masters of king, lords, commons, and priests."[25] Here was revolutionary doctrine, indeed, the sort of talk to drive a sharp wedge between members of the different social classes.

Among conservatives of this period none expressed his views on the social problems of the times more fully or more often than did Jonathan Boucher, the Tory parson of Maryland. In a sermon in 1773, he asserted that "there never was a time when a whole people were so little governed by settled good principles." The evil was not confined simply to affairs of government but extended to "every department of society":

Parents complain, and not without reason, that children are no longer so respectful and dutiful as they ought to be, and as they used to be; whilst children might, with no less reason, object to their parents' still more culpable instances of a failure of duty. Both employers and the employed, much to their mutual shame and inconvenience, no longer live together with anything like attachment and cordiality on either side; and the laboring classes, instead of regarding the rich as their guardians, patrons, and benefactors,

[24] *Ibid.*, pp. 74–75.
[25] Schlesinger, *Colonial Merchants and the American Revolution*, p. 433, citing Newport *Mercury*, September 26, 1774, and *Pinckney's Virginia Gazette*, October 13, 1774.

now look on them as so many overgrown colossuses, whom it is no demerit in them to wrong. A still more general (and it is to be feared no less just) topic of complaint is, that the lower classes, instead of being industrious, frugal, and orderly (virtues so peculiarly becoming their station in life), are become idle, improvident, and dissolute.[26]

Boucher, like many another conservative, was distrustful of the popularity seeker and especially of the man who tried to sway the masses by his oratory. His curate once preached a "silly" republican sermon which contributed "to blow the coals of sedition." Boucher was furious that the man had so demeaned himself for the sake of popularity, "for to be very popular it is, I believe, necessary to be very like the bulk of the people, that is, wrongheaded, ignorant, and prone to resist authority." The rector was persuaded that "whenever it happens that a really sensible man becomes the idol of the people, it must be owing to his possessing a talent of letting himself down to their level."[27] John Randolph, the Loyalist attorney general of Virginia, had likewise "ever held in contempt the applause of a giddy multitude." He refused, he said, to call a man a patriot *because* he enjoyed the acclamations of the people. "The populace, from freak or interest, are ever ready to elevate their leader to the pinnacle of fame; and experience informs us that they are as ready to pull him down." Those who were "running the race of popularity," he went on, "whilst they are the greatest sticklers for the liberty of others, are themselves the most abject slaves in politics. They have no opinion of their own, but are the echo of the people. Propriety and wisdom are often abandoned, in order to pursue the wills of their noisy constituents." Many men who had been held up in their day as "spotless patriots had,

---

[26] Boucher, *American Revolution*, pp. 309–10.
[27] Boucher, *Reminiscences*, p. 119.

nevertheless, in the historian's pages, when truth triumphed over delusion, been pronounced the assassins of liberty."[28]

Scorn of the lower classes, distrust of those who sought to play upon the emotions of the masses, and fear that the "mechanics and country clowns" would come to take a place in society rightfully belonging only to "the people of property, of best sense and character": these were motives influencing the final position of many members of the colonial aristocracy. They believed sincerely that the guidance of public affairs was the natural responsibility of gentlemen and of gentlemen alone. They had inherited from England the principle of social stratification and they had been reared in a tradition of leadership. With John Randolph they held in all honesty to the notion that "the ignorant vulgar are as unfit to judge of the modes, as they are unable to manage the reins, of government."[29] Quite apart from any question of self-interest (or at least so they thought) the aristocrats looked with alarm upon the appearance of a more democratic spirit and believed that colonial society was suffering from a nearly fatal illness. This attitude, sincerely held by many of the gentry of the time and not unknown in similar circles even today, was a leading reason why numbers of colonists decided to throw their support to Britain. It seemed clear to them at last that only British authority, backed up by British arms if necessary, could cure the disease with which America was afflicted. Only thus could the social balance be restored to its true level.

After the war began, the social issue seemed even more clearly drawn. Men of no great social position, the Sam Adams', the

[28] Earl G. Swem, ed., *Considerations of the Present State of Virginia, Attributed to John Randolph, Attorney-General, and, Considerations of the Present State of Virginia Examined by Robert Carter Nicholas, 1774* (New York: Charles F. Heartman, 1919) pp. 15, 17–18 (hereafter cited as [Randolph], *Considerations on the Present State of Virginia*).
[29] *Ibid.*, p. 15.

Patrick Henrys, gained even more authority than before. In spite of the views of aristocratic officers like Washington, many commissions in the American Army went to men of little property and of uncouth manners. The terms "officer" and "gentleman" were not necessarily synonymous. What was worse, wealthy and cultivated Loyalists were subject to physical mistreatment, and when they fled for safety their property was confiscated. The war seemed to many to have destroyed the last vestiges of social decency and order.

Not all aristocrats, of course, joined the British; those who cast their lot wholly with the American cause sometimes had to swallow their pride and accept as gracefully as they could treatment which must have been revolting to their sense of social propriety. Thomas Anburey, a British officer in Burgoyne's captured army who has left an interesting description of phases of American life during the Revolution, had a chance to observe the sadly democratizing influence which the war had on plantation society and the reaction of one gentleman to the situation. While he was at the Virginia home of Colonel Randolph of Tuckahoe, "three country peasants, who came upon business, entered the room where the colonel and his company were sitting." Unbidden, they "took themselves chairs, drew near the fire, began spitting, pulling off their country boots all over mud, and then opened their business." When the unpleasant callers had finally left, someone commented on the great liberties they had taken. Their host replied with some bitterness that "it was unavoidable, the spirit of independency was converted into equality, and everyone who bore arms esteemed himself upon a footing with his neighbor." Randolph's final remark is not only a footnote on the effect of the war upon the common people; it is even more an illuminating commentary on the social attitude of the aristocratic colonel. "No doubt," he concluded, and we can imagine the indignation he threw into the words, "each of these men conceives himself, in every respect, my equal."[30]

When peace came at last, that impossible, incredible peace, in which the "disorderly" forces of American society were triumphant, the Loyalist aristocrats feared that the world as they had known it was gone forever. Whether those who had fled returned or stayed in exile, no lasting good could come from a system in which social distinctions were lost and the lower classes prevailed. Yet some who had gone but still loved America had a little hope left. They wanted to return not only for their own sakes but because they thought that men of their class would be needed to re-create a stabilizing and conserving force. One such was Samuel Curwen, admiralty judge of Massachusetts, who had gone to England early in the war. Writing from London to a friend in Salem in August 1783, he expressed his ardent wish that moderate councils might prevail and that there might be no "illiberal, impolitic exclusion of all absentees." For himself he seemed not greatly to care; he was too old to do much in the rebuilding of his own life. But he was far from indifferent to what he considered "the real welfare of America," and he was free to declare his apprehension "that the lower, illiterate classes, narrow-minded and illiberal all over the world, [would] have too much influence" in the new nation.[31] If that nation was to gain any semblance of stability, thought Judge Curwen and many others like him, men of the upper social ranks, including the former Loyalists, must be restored to social and political leadership. Such men had a clear notion of the social implications of the recent struggle but they were not yet ready to accept the verdict. The exile, who is himself the first sufferer, is apt to be the last convert to the principles of a revolution.

[30] [Anburey], *Travels through the Interior Parts of America*, pp. 370–71.

[31] George A. Ward, ed., *Journal and Letters of the Late Samuel Curwen, Judge of Admiralty, etc., an American Refugee in England, from 1775 to 1784* . . . . (New York and Boston, 1842), p. 387.

A BALANCED GOVERNMENT

"Our constitution of government," wrote Cadwallader Colden of New York, "is nearly the same with that which the people of England value so much that they have at all times cheerfully hazarded their lives in the support of it . . . . and therefore it seems evident to me that it is most prudent in us to keep as near as possible to that plan which our mother country has for so many ages experienced to be best and which has been preserved at such vast expense of blood and treasure." [1] In these words Colden expressed the fundamental point of view of the colonial conservative on all aspects of political theory. The constitution of the mother country was the model for that of every colony, and the governmental system that was desirable for the one was equally desirable for the other.

In considering the political philosophy of the colonists, whether conservative or radical, the essential fact to bear in mind is that it was almost wholly British in its origins and drew upon English history for its justification. It is true that the best-educated colonists were familiar with the history of Greece and Rome and signed many of their letters to the newspapers with such classical pseudonyms as "Cato," "Philo Patriae," or "Publicus." There is little evidence, however, to show that the colonists were much influenced in their theories of the ideal state by their knowledge of practices in Athens, in Sparta, or in Rome. The examples of classical antiquity became important

[1] *Letters and Papers of Cadwallader Colden*, IX, 251.

only after the Americans had declared their independence and were creating new frames of government for themselves.

Likewise the history of continental Europe and the works of Italian and French writers had little direct influence upon political thinking in the colonies. Machiavelli was known to many but his concept of the state was almost wholly alien to the American tradition and his ideas were uncongenial to the American atmosphere. They gained no foothold over here. The French political theorists of the Age of the Enlightenment were quite widely read, especially Rousseau and Montesquieu, and an occasional historian has asserted that they had an important formative influence on the opinions of such men as Thomas Jefferson. The fact remains, however, that for all practical purposes, as far as the American colonies were concerned, the political ideas of these Frenchmen seemed largely to be derived from contemplation of the British constitution and to reflect principles already laid down by British authors. Americans did not need to import at secondhand theories which were already a part of their own British heritage. Such men as Harrington, Locke, and Blackstone not only wrote in the colonists' own language but they spoke in a political idiom that was familiar. So far as it can properly be said that any one group of writers "influenced" political theory in the colonies it was these Englishmen, and especially John Locke, who played the most immediate and most significant roles.

There was more involved, however, in the conditioning of American political thought than the writings of a few men. In fact, it can be confidently stated that none of them would have had any important influence if the ideas they represented were not already congenial to the political atmosphere in America. That atmosphere resulted in large part from the fact that the colonists were chiefly of English stock and had behind them the same heritage of English history and English political experience that constituted the background out of which Locke and his fellow theorists developed their ideas. One of the chief criticisms that can justly be leveled, it seems to me, against some of our present-day teachers and writers on the history of political theory is that too often they present the great figures — Plato, Machiavelli, Marx, or any others — without giving full attention to the historical context in which these men wrote. There is little use, I believe, in trying to understand Plato's *Republic* without first understanding the political system under which Plato lived and which, in considerable part, he hoped to reform. It makes little sense, historically at any rate, to present Karl Marx without fully and fairly examining the society of Western Europe in the mid-nineteenth century and analyzing the events that had disturbed the economic and social foundations on which it rested. Political theory can profitably be studied only in its proper context.

That context for the American colonists in the hundred years leading up to independence was a mixture of British and American experience and political practice. Everything that was a part of that experience influenced their reception of the views of political theorists; everything in their own political practices contributed positively or negatively, directly or indirectly, to their own attitudes and to their actions. Other things were relatively unimportant. It is, therefore, in the light of their English background and their mixed British and American history that the political theories of the colonists must be understood.

When Englishmen or colonists of the eighteenth century looked back on the seventeenth they were confronted with the fact that two political revolutions had taken place. One of these had cost Charles I his head; the other had driven James II from his throne. Superficially, the two events might seem to have much in common; each had struck a heavy blow at the monarchy; each had involved the principle of resistance to established authority. And yet, as the great majority of Englishmen of the next century viewed them, the two revolutions were vastly different. In the case of the first, after the chief grievances had been redressed, a small minority had seized power and driven all other factions out of office. They had then destroyed the monarchy itself and set up what purported to be a republican commonwealth but one which soon degenerated into a dictatorship. The second revolution had driven a king into exile and had given strength to the parliamentary branch of government at royal expense but had by no means destroyed the principle of monarchy itself. The conflict had, in fact, led to the establishment of that line of kings to which every good Englishman in the eighteenth century gave allegiance. What was, as a practical matter, an even greater difference in men's retrospective attitudes was that the first revolution had ultimately failed but the second had succeeded. Not only had Charles II been restored to his ancestral throne after the collapse of the Protectorate, but most Englishmen of the next century repudiated many of the very principles — political, social, and religious — upon which much of Cromwell's system had been based. The Revolution of 1688, on the other hand, had prevailed. It had been maintained in the face of foreign war and domestic uprising and had laid the foundation of England's political system for generations to come. It was, in short, a "Glorious Revolution."

Inevitably, those who accepted the results of the Revolution of 1688 — and they constituted the vast majority of Englishmen in both the mother country and the colonies — believed in the principles upon which it was based. They considered those writers who served as its apologists to be the ultimate authority on political philosophy. Among those writers, none stood so high in the estimation of succeeding generations as did John Locke. The theories he expounded justified the Revolution and became the political dogma of the eighteenth-century Englishman. In those parts of his work which are relevant to our present theme, Locke asserted that society was founded on natural law; that government was based in the first instance upon consent; that men in a state of nature had agreed for their mutual good to submit to a common authority; and that with that authority (in this case the king) they had made a compact, binding on both sides, under which the ruler was to govern according to principles of justice and in the interest of public welfare, and the governed were to give their obedience. If, however, the ruler overstepped the bounds of authority agreed upon, he thereby violated his contract and the people were automatically released from the obligations imposed upon them.

This was by no means a new theory; its essential parts can be traced back through the writings of many centuries. But, as elaborated and expounded by Locke, it was well suited to the English temperament and it was particularly useful as a justification of the uprising against James II. It was easy to demonstrate to the general satisfaction that that monarch had been the first to break the compact.

Locke's theories had wide currency not only in England but also in America. In fact, as Professor McLaughlin has pointed out, some of the colonies could even be cited as living proofs of the truth of Locke's contentions.[2] Had they not themselves been founded on mutual compacts before that philosopher was even born? What was the Mayflower Compact, what the plantation covenants of the New England towns, what the church covenants of the Congregationalists, but cases of men coming

[2] Andrew C. McLaughlin's volume in the Anson G. Phelps Lectureship series, *The Foundations of American Constitutionalism* (New York: New York University Press, 1932), is an invaluable treatment of the importance of the compact theory in early America. On the aspects of the subject especially pertinent to the present theme, see the first three chapters.

together in a state of nature and agreeing upon certain governmental systems under which they would live in peace and harmony? What were the various "Concessions and Agreements," "Frames of Government," and "Fundamental Constitutions" of the proprietary colonies (one of which Locke himself had helped to draft) but compacts between lords and people under which colonists agreed to settle in the wilderness and submit to proprietary rule? Surely no one in America could look back upon the century of settlement without seeing there plentiful examples of just that sort of compact and consent which Locke said was the origin of all civil government.

The theory of compact was especially useful in explaining and supporting the English government of the eighteenth century and the Hanoverian dynasty, established as these were on the foundations of a revolution and threatened from time to time by efforts to restore the Stuart line. It was very convenient to be able to say that James II had broken the contract and that the English people had made a new agreement and were now living under a government based on their full consent. This argument did very well when all was going smoothly or when the only threat to government came from the small minority of disgruntled Jacobites. But what if other men became dissatisfied with the existing scheme of things and declared that the government now in power had violated the new compact between rulers and the ruled, or asserted that they had not given their consent to the current exercise of power? Then the "right of revolution" and the "appeal to heaven" which had figured so largely in the language of 1688 might become embarrassing indeed. The very theories which had justified that revolution might be used to start another. Fortunately for those in control, no really serious danger arose within England, except from supporters of the Stuarts, during the period we are dealing with. But trouble did appear in the colonies, and those who objected to British policy began to turn the pages of Locke and to cite the great philosopher in justification of their disobedience. Then the upholders of the government, those in America as well as those in England, found the compact theory a little trying; suddenly the great "revolution principles" required a bit of fresh explaining.

During the first six decades of the eighteenth century there had been little controversy in America over questions of political philosophy. In each colony nearly all men of any consequence accepted the same basic principles and differed only on practical details or, occasionally, on the extent to which those basic principles should be carried into effective force. But when the problem of the relation of the colonies to the mother country became acute, then more fundamental differences arose. While most writers and orators of both sides ostensibly supported the same theories, each emphasized different aspects of the philosophy by which the British system was justified. Champions of the "radical" colonial position stressed the ideas of compact and of the limitations upon authority; advocates of the "conservative" British position considered far more important the concept of balance between the elements of a political society and the necessity of obedience to duly constituted government. Doubtless both sides indulged somewhat in rationalizing and used theories as convenient weapons without inquiring too closely into their intrinsic soundness; but both sides likewise based their theoretical expositions upon attitudes and assumptions that were fundamental to the men who used them.

Among the conservatives a very few were extreme enough to repudiate the whole theory of compact. Of such men our old friend Jonathan Boucher was the frankest in taking a thoroughly Jacobite and high-Tory position. In a letter to an English friend in 1773, he expressed his horror at the theories being taught to American college students. A youth at Princeton, he had heard, delivered a commencement oration declaring that government was derived from a compact between king and people; that if either partly failed to live up to the stipulated conditions, the compact became void; and that King George, by consenting to laws oppressive to America, "had violated the conditions and therefore forfeited all title to allegiance." These were "principles subversive of all good government," said Boucher,[3] and he soon addressed himself to their refutation.

In a sermon on "Civil Liberty; Passive Obedience, and Non-Resistance," he attacked the fundamental assumptions underlying the theories of Locke and his followers.[4] He denied that government had originally been established by common consent, for that notion implies the ideas that the end of all government is the common good, and that men can and do agree on what constitutes the common good. These ideas Boucher questioned. Furthermore, the theory of consent rests on the notion of the equality of the human race. But the very nature of government requires relative superiority and inferiority among the members of an organized society. Hence the establishment of government by consent would destroy the equality upon which it theoretically rests, unless men, to preserve their equality, reserve the right to withdraw their consent to government whenever they see fit. Social life, in that case, would be reduced "to the wearisome, confused, and useless task of mankind's first expressing then withdrawing their consent to an endless succession of schemes of government." For himself Boucher would

[3] "Letters of Rev. Jonathan Boucher," *Maryland Historical Magazine*, VIII (1913), 183–84.

[4] Boucher, *American Revolution*, pp. 495–560, especially pp. 512–18. This sermon, preached in 1775, was specifically a reply to one by the Reverend Jacob Duché, one of the few Anglican clergymen of Pennsylvania to espouse the American side in the early years of the controversy. Boucher's statement of the Lockian theory is largely based on Duché's contemporary exposition of that theory.

avoid the whole difficulty by denying the inherent equality of mankind. Men, he said, differ from each other in everything that can be supposed to lead to supremacy and subjection, "*as one star differs from another star in glory*." Thus he would likewise deny the theory of consent.

If Locke and his followers try to avoid this difficulty, said the Maryland minister, by arguing that every individual on entering the social compact has first actively agreed to be bound in all cases by the majority, they are still abandoning the principle of equality and, furthermore, they contradict themselves in another direction. Locke preaches that a right of resistance exists in the governed, and what is resistance to an established government but a withdrawal of consent to be ruled by the will of the majority as expressed in laws? Thus Boucher, more realistic than many American conservatives, saw that the compact theory involved inadequacies and contradictions. He believed that it would lead in practice to anarchy. He saw, too, that the theories which had justified one revolution might be used to support another. As he remarked on another occasion, the friends of William III and of the Hanoverians had been very shortsighted in laying so much stress on the doctrines of compact and consent.[5]

Few if any of Boucher's fellow colonists attacked so directly the basic theories expounded by John Locke, but a number joined with him in urging the importance of passive obedience and nonresistance. In many cases their position was based on religious principle quite as much as upon political theory. The Quakers and some of the German sects of Pennsylvania were, of course, notable for their acceptance of a wholly passive attitude toward the forceful exercise of governmental authority.

[5] In a sermon of 1775 on "The Dispute Between the Israelites and the Two Tribes and A Half, Respecting Their Settlement Beyond Jordan," *ibid.*, pp. 484–85.

The Quaker testimony in favor of obedience and submission became particularly important in the period just before the Revolution. In 1774, for example, a group of Philadelphians, who declared that they included members of all denominations in the city, published a plea for the closing of all business houses on the day the Boston Port Act went into effect. The Quaker leaders of the city protested. For themselves and the various Friends' Meetings in the city, they announced that any Quakers who might have supported the proposed demonstration had "manifested great inattention to our religious principles and profession and acted contrary to the rules of Christian discipline established .... among us."[6] Not even by such a mild and peaceable method of demonstration as the closing of all shops for a day ought the good Quaker to show resistance to constituted authority.

During the same period many Anglican clergymen helped to support the royal government by preaching the doctrine of passive obedience and nonresistance. They devoted themselves in public and in private, as the Reverend Ebenezer Diblee of Stamford, Connecticut, put it, to inculcating "the great duty of obedience and subjection to the government in being."[7]

While Anglican ministers in nearly all the colonies were taking this position on religious as well as political grounds, it remained again for Boucher to state the case for nonresistance most completely. He made clear his position in a series of four sermons which together constitute the best and fullest exposition of what were the essentially Tory principles of obedience and nonresistance produced in colonial America.[8] All govern-

[6] Lincoln, *Revolutionary Movement in Pennsylvania*, p. 168, quoting *The Pennsylvania Gazette*, June 1, 1774.

[7] Hawks and Perry, *Documentary History*, II, 85.

[8] "On Fundamental Principles," 1773, Boucher, *American Revolution*, pp. 294–324; "On the Character of Achitophel," 1774, *ibid.*, pp. 402–34; "The Dispute Between the Israelites and the Two Tribes and A Half,

ment, he declared, must by its very nature be absolute and irresistible. It cannot be limited even by itself or it loses the essential quality of supremacy and so destroys itself. To resist government is therefore to destroy its very essence. Every man who is a subject must necessarily owe to the government under which he lives an obedience which is either active or passive. In those cases where political duty does not conflict with conscience, obedience should be active. In those cases where the performance required is forbidden by God, then obedience should be passive; that is, the subject should not perform the required act but should patiently "submit to the penalties annexed to disobedience." A man of good principles, one resolute not to disobey God, ought to determine, in case of competition, to disobey man, such an act being the lesser of the two evils; but he knows that if he should fail at the same time to submit patiently to the penalties incurred by his disobedience to man, he would be disobeying God also. In no case ought he to offer resistance to the orders of government. This was the principle of passive obedience.

To speak of nonresistance as some men did as involving "continued submission to violence" was, in Boucher's opinion, inaccurate. For he did not believe that in a lawful government there could be, properly speaking, any such thing as violence. The decrees and acts of lawful government might be unwise, severe, and even oppressive, but he did not see how they could be called "violence." In a political sense he would apply the term only to the exercise of power by persons not legally invested with power, however necessary, humane, and beneficent their acts might be. These were true acts of violence and to resist them was altogether right. On the other hand, said

Respecting Their Settlement Beyond Jordan," 1775, *ibid.*, pp. 450–94; "On Civil Liberty; Passive Obedience, and Non-Resistance," 1775, *ibid.*, pp. 495–560.

Boucher, it was a *"damnable doctrine and position* that any government lawfully established may be denounced or resisted by any self-commissioned persons invested with no authority by law, *on any pretense whatsoever."* [9] The doctrine of nonresistance which Boucher expounded at such length was summarized in one sentence by William Eddis, a royal customs officer in Maryland, when he said: "Surely, in a moral point of view, it is highly criminal to attempt, by unjust or indirect methods, to obtain a redress [even] of the most oppressive grievances." [10]

These theories, based partly on religious grounds and partly on purely political principles, represented the extreme conservative view both in England and in America. This was the position taken by the supporters of James II at the time of the Revolution of 1688, and it continued to be the high-Tory position in the eighteenth century. It did not find much support among the bulk of the colonial conservatives. Most of these men had been reared in a Whig rather than a Tory tradition and were unwilling to reject the political theories of the English Revolution. Besides, Boucher's position was essentially a negative one, denying the principles of compact and consent and advocating passive obedience and nonresistance. Most colonial conservatives, on the other hand, cast their ideas as far as possible in essentially positive terms. They stressed the virtues of the British constitution, of the balance of power it exemplified, and the value to the colonists of the British connection. In emphasizing these points they found it necessary to denounce certain tendencies of the radicals, but their position was basically that of men who were urging the preservation of a political system in which they positively believed.

Throughout the colonies, until almost the very end, the vast

[9] *Ibid.*, p. 483. The italics are Boucher's.

[10] William Eddis, *Letters from America, Historical and Descriptive; Comprising Occurrences from 1769, to 1777, Inclusive* (London, 1792), p. 166.

majority of those who wrote and spoke on political subjects expressed their deep admiration for the British constitution. Liberals and conservatives united to declare it the finest, freest, most perfect system existing anywhere for human government. Although the radicals came to believe that the constitution had been perverted by the men in power, they seldom failed to express their devotion to what they considered its true principles. It was, they insisted, the violation of these principles to which they took exception. Only after the conflict had reached the point of open warfare did any but those on the extreme "left" wing seriously question the soundness of the constitution itself. The conservatives, for their part, emphasized throughout the glories of the British system and argued that if it was being perverted, the radicals, not the ministry, were the guilty party. If the colonists would only stop and think, they would realize what grandeur they were so lightly threatening to destroy.

The constitutional principle which the conservatives most heavily emphasized was that of balance. We have been taught in our day to think of a "balanced government" or a system of "checks and balances" as involving a sound division of power between the three great functional branches of government— the executive, the legislative, and the judicial. In the British and colonial governments of the eighteenth century the idea of balance was applied with far less emphasis on the corresponding functional organs of the state—the king and his ministers, the two houses of Parliament, and the courts—than it was on the sources of political power and on the consequent nature of the state. Great Britain, men never tired of repeating, was a "mixed monarchy," neither a despotism nor a democracy. The constitution of the eighteenth century, as one colonial conservative put it, consisted "in a proper balance between the monarchical, aristocratical, and democratical forms of government."[11] We

---

[11] *Letters and Papers of Cadwallader Colden*, IX, 251.

might liken the state, as these men saw it, to a three-legged stool, held upright by its three supporting members, the king, the aristocracy, and the people at large. As long as the three legs were equal the stool would provide a firm and level seat of government. If one limb were weakened the whole structure would lose its basic strength; if one limb were made too long, the seat would no longer be level, its center of gravity would be disturbed, and it would provide at best only a precarious support. Equality of the members was essential to perfect balance.

As men of British stock, in the colonies as well as in England, looked back over their long history, they believed they could see the perfect illustration of the importance of balance between the three great sources of strength in the constitution. For English history furnished convincing examples of situations both of balance and of the lack of it. One of the most interesting summaries of English history from this point of view was written about 1745 by Cadwallader Colden, a conservative political leader of New York, in an essay entitled "Observations on the Balance of Power in Government."[12] The English government, he wrote, had not always been well balanced. After the Norman Conquest, monarchy had had too great weight, democracy too little; the barons were the only check upon the crown. The Barons' Wars had reduced the royal power, only in turn to upset the balance in favor of the aristocracy. Henry VII had used the commons to bring redress, and never since — note this — never since had the constitution been endangered by the "aristocratical" part. Under Henry VIII royal power had

---

[12] *Ibid.*, pp. 251–57. In this paper Colden was for the most part simply restating the ideas of a host of English political theorists of his own and earlier generations. For a summary of the principle as expounded in England during the seventeenth and eighteeth centuries, see Stanley Pargellis, "The Theory of Balanced Government," in Conyers Read, ed., *The Constitution Reconsidered* (New York: Columbia University Press, 1938), pp. 37–49.

again become too great. Only the circumstance that the later Tudors who succeeded him were a weak boy, Edward VI, and two women, Mary and Elizabeth, and that the first of the Stuarts, King James, was a "weak, timid prince" had prevented the firm establishment of absolutism. In Charles I's time the barons had been too feeble to withstand the crown so they had thrown their weight on the side of the commons. But "this was done so inconsiderately," said Colden, that the balance had tipped too far in favor of the commons, and the whole constitution was overthrown by Cromwell and the Puritans. Anarchy, then tyranny, then absolutism had followed. Happily, however, a change took place and with the great events of 1688 and 1689 the true and perfect balance between the three elements had been restored.

Many other writers elaborated on this general theme. Among the most explicit was John Randolph, attorney general of Virginia. True patriotism, he asserted, consisted not in a separate attachment to any particular branch of government, but in preserving the three elements "in that degree of strength and vigor which the constitution intends that each shall enjoy." The king's power exists "to secure his person from insult, to allow him all the pageantry of dignity, and to strengthen his hand in the doing good, but by no means to admit of his doing wrong. To answer these purposes the executive power is placed under his direction." The people have a share of power which is exercised for them by their representatives since the populace is too numerous to act directly. These representatives, the "fiduciaries to the people," must consent only to such laws as are to the advantage of the community; they must "secure the persons of their constituents from unreasonable pains and penalties," and safeguard the people's property against unjust seizure. The lords are an intermediate state. Like Janus they look two ways, forward to see that the king does not infringe the people's rights, backward to observe that the people do not overstep their privileges. "There are, within every government, many interior movements," as in a clock, "but in England, the united power of king, lords, and commons is the great wheel by which all the others are brought into motion and action." The great Governor of the Earth, Randolph went on, changing his figure of speech, takes care that all the world's decays and excrescences are at once corrected. "Rulers in polity below" should imitate this pattern and preserve all the constituent parts of government entire. If a man in authority would "allow to the king what is his just prerogative, and take from the people what does not belong to them; would look minutely into those departments with which they are more intimately connected, and, without favor or prejudice, keep the society moving on its proper hinges; such a man, and such only, I would call a patriot, or friend to his country."[13]

The relation of this theory of mixed monarchy to the colonies was clear. Again and again both theorists and practical politicians pointed out that the three elements of king, lords, and commons were represented on a smaller scale in each province by governor, council, and assembly. If the colonists were to preserve for themselves the excellencies of the British constitution, they must take care to maintain the same true balance between the three branches as existed in the mother country. When the more liberal members of the assembly advanced this argument, they used it to support the claims of the lower house to all the privileges and powers of the House of Commons. But when royal officers or conservative colonials talked about preserving the balance they always meant that the people or their elected representatives were threatening to upset it at the expense of the royal or aristocratic elements of the pro-

[13] [Randolph], *Considerations on the Present State of Virginia*, pp. 18–19.

vincial constitution. As so often happens, it was in the application of the theory that essential differences appeared.

Colden, the New York aristocrat, was frank to say that in his reading of history "mixed government" ran much more risk from too great power in the "monarchical" or "democratical" than in the "aristocratical" part, and, between the first two, the danger of popular excess was far the greater "because people are always jealous of the monarch but fond of everything that increases the democracy." So it was in the colonial polity. The royal governor had no power without money, which he could get only from the assembly. The council, representing the colonial aristocracy, could "never be an overmatch for any one of the other two parts of our constitution." The governor, on his part, could suspend councilors, and they had to rely on his authority to put their schemes in execution. Like the governor they depended on the assembly for money, while like the members of the lower house they were colonists with estates and families here and could never be conceived of as joining with the governor to lessen the liberties and privileges of the people of the province. The council certainly was not dangerous. What dangers there were to a true balance came only from the assembly, which by controlling finance and by other methods might reduce the power of the other branches to an unhealthy level.[14]

James Duane, a New York conservative who ultimately sided with the colonies, was one of the many who agreed with Colden that no danger could possibly come from too great power in the hands of the colonial aristocracy. In fact, Duane would have gone even further and would have strengthened the middle branch by giving life tenure to the councilors. He regretted that there was no American peerage, as his biographer has put it, "to

[14] *Letters and Papers of Cadwallader Colden*, IX, 252–54.

serve as a shock-absorber between prince and people."[15] William Eddis, the Maryland official, was somewhat more specific. Writing in 1770, he pointed out that if an order of nobility had been created at an early period in America and bishops had been appointed "it would most assuredly have greatly tended to cherish a steady adherence to monarchical principles and have more strongly riveted the attachment of the colonies to the present state." It was because of "inattention to principles of such importance," he thought, that America had given birth to sentiments "totally repugnant to the genius of our most excellent constitution."[16]

Joseph Galloway of Pennsylvania was another who took a similar position on the importance of an aristocratic element in the governmental system of America. He defended the Massachusetts Government Act of 1774, which took from the assembly of that colony the right of electing councilors. The former absence of an aristocratic appointive element in the Massachusetts system, he said, had produced notorious mischiefs. The British constitution required "an independent, aristocratical authority" between king and people, "able to throw its weight in either scale as the other should preponderate." By this policy alone the freedom of the British government had endured for ages past and only by such a policy could it be maintained for ages yet to come. The right of creating such an aristocratic part was fixed in the Crown; the people had never claimed it, and no king had ever been authorized to give it away. It was preposterous that this royal power had ever been surrendered to the assembly in Massachusetts, and as he thought it over Galloway grew violent. The charter before amendment, he sputtered, "was manifestly calculated to efface all the laws, habits, man-

[15] Edward P. Alexander, *A Revolutionary Conservative, James Duane of New York* (New York: Columbia University Press, 1938), p. 97.
[16] Eddis, *Letters from America*, pp. 51–53.

ners, and opinions which it ought to support, to destroy that system of polity which it ought to have maintained, and to level all the orders, arrangements, checks, and balances, wisely graduated and tempered, of a mixed monarchy, to the lowest and most imperfect of all political systems, a tumultuous, seditious, and inert democracy." Far from causing alarm to America, the revocation of this charter privilege in Massachusetts should bring satisfaction to all right-thinking people and ought to be followed by similar measures for other colonies, "till every colonial charter is made conformable to the true fundamental principles of a mixed monarchy."[17]

It was partly because of this apparent lack of a truly aristocratic branch in the constitutions of the New England colonies (with the exception of New Hampshire) that some conservatives felt such antipathy to that section. To this view Colden was somewhat of an exception. Although he showed his dislike for the "republicanism" of the New England Puritans, he did not conceal his surprise at observing "how well the magistrates keep up the dignity of their offices, with what strictness and even sometimes with what severity they put their laws in execution, notwithstanding that their authority expires annually and that they hold their offices at the good liking of the people they govern." This example, he thought, showed the degree to which authority depended on good discipline, a quality which Massachusetts and Connecticut, at least, seemed to him to possess.[18]

[17] [Joseph Galloway], *Historical and Political Reflections on the Rise and Progress of the American Rebellion* (London, 1780), pp. 19–23, 31–32.

[18] "Account of the Government of the New England Colonies" (*ca.* 1742), *Letters and Papers of Cadwallader Colden*, IX, 247. Colden goes on to remark the regularity of re-election of magistrates in Massachusetts and Connecticut: "Seldom are their officers changed while they strictly support the government and execute their laws, and the offices for the most part continue in the same families from father to son."

But most non-Puritan observers of the conservative school agreed with Galloway that the constitutions of New England were impossibly republican. From Connecticut itself the Anglican Samuel Johnson, later the first president of King's College, declared that the government there was "much too popular" and that it was under a "Junto rule," whereby a small clique held the offices in return for allowing the people to live and act as they pleased.[19] From farther off the republicanism of New England seemed just as outrageous as it did from within the section. Boucher believed that "the people of the four New England governments may challenge the whole world to produce another people who, without actually rebelling, have, throughout their whole history, been so disaffected to government, so uniformly intolerant towards all who differ from them, so dissatisfied and disorderly, and in short, so impatient under every proper legal restraint not imposed by themselves."[20] Men of a conservative point of view were not yet ready to shift the balance in favor of the "democratical" element in government at the expense of the "aristocratical."

Nor, for that matter, were most of them willing to go far to curtail the royal element, at least in so far as it involved a reasonably strong executive in America. Landon Carter of Virginia observed in his diary that a republican system was just as likely to produce arbitrary government as a limited monarchy, and "necessity is no better a plea" for the introduction of arbitrary rule "in a republican form than it is or can be in a monarchical form."[21] Many of the royal governors wrote back to England

---

Ibid., pp. 247–48. For some statistical analysis bearing out Colden's observation, see above, pp. 21–26.

[19] H. and C. Schneider, *Samuel Johnson*, I, 149–50. See also p. 349.

[20] Boucher, *American Revolution*, p. 474.

[21] Entry of May 23, 1776, "Diary of Col. Landon Carter," *William and Mary Quarterly*, 1st Series, XVIII (July 1909), 39.

that the home government was weakening the colonial executives by depriving them of sufficient patronage to give their positions weight.[22] A similar warning was addressed to the people of Maryland: "Deprive your king or your governor," a clergyman wrote, "of all means of benefiting others, and, unless you should see fit to restore prerogative . . . . you deprive him of his proper share of weight in the scale of government." With all the advantages of family connection and of control of the purse on the colonists' side, "the preponderance of the two houses when opposed to the kingly power, would be, in comparison, as the measure of a mountain is to that of a molehill." By lessening the prestige of the persons employed in high offices of government, the people would "clip the wings of the most conspicuous and dignified branch of government."[23]

As far back as 1716 Caleb Heathcote of New York advocated the establishment of a permanent revenue fund as a means of making the executive independent of the assembly. Were such a system of taxation established throughout the colonies, he told the Treasury Board in England, it would render "great satisfaction in having all governors and other officers receive their bread and support from the hands of the king, without a slavish dependence for it on the uncertain humors of assemblies."[24] American history might have taken a very different course if Heathcote's advice had been followed at the time.

[22] Leonard W. Labaree, *Royal Government in America* (New Haven: Yale University Press, 1930), pp. 102–7.

[23] Boucher, *American Revolution*, pp. 218–19. After the Revolution had begun he wrote the undersecretary of state for the colonies urging that, following reconquest of the colonies, their governments should be "new modeled" to give "some pith and energy" to the executive branch. "Letters of Rev. Jonathan Boucher," *Maryland Historical Magazine*, VII (September 1913), 247.

[24] Dixon Ryan Fox, *Caleb Heathcote, Gentleman Colonist; the Story of a Career in the Province of New York* (New York: Charles Scribner's Sons, 1926), p. 181.

In general, conservatives tended to brand as "republican" or "democratical" any tendency to shift the balance in favor of the popular element at the expense of the aristocratic or royal branches of government. They used "republican" and "democratical" almost synonymously and considered them as terms of reproach, much as in the social sphere they used the adjective "leveling" and as most present-day Americans use "red" and "Communist." Popular governments were weak governments, according to Boucher, and Colden looked with dismay upon any system in which important questions of state rested on the votes of men of "little credit or reputation."[25] Alexander Graydon, an aristocratic Philadelphian, later a Federalist, reflected the general attitude of the conservative eighteenth-century American, both before and after the Revolution, when, in attacking the "republican maxim of *vox populi vox dei*," he quoted with relish and approval these lines from Milton:

> And what the people, but a herd confus'd,
> A miscellaneous rabble, who extol
> Things vulgar, and well weigh'd, scarce worth the praise!
> They praise and they admire they know not what;
> And know not whom, but as one leads the other;
> And what delight to be by such extolled,
> To live upon their tongues and be their talk,
> Of whom to be despised were no small praise.[26]

Conservative Americans, as has been said, seemed more disturbed at the possibility that the popular element would upset the balance of government than at the thought that such a move

---

[25] Boucher, *American Revolution*, p. lvii; *Letters and Papers of Cadwallader Colden*, IX, 355.

[26] [Alexander Graydon], *Memoirs of a Life, Chiefly Passed in Pennsylvania, within the Last Sixty Years* (Harrisburgh, 1811), pp. 305–6. The lines quoted are from *Paradise Regained*, Bk. III, ll. 49–56. They are printed here in the form in which Graydon gives them. In the final line, "despised" should read "dispraised."

would come from either of the other two branches. In this respect they differed from men of more liberal stamp, who feared particularly what they considered to be encroachments by the executive. The more radical also began to feel that wealth and breeding should give no man a special place in government as a member of an aristocracy. Men of all schools of thought had been brought up in the tradition of a balanced government, but they could not agree as to which of the three branches was the most likely in their own day to usurp too great a share of power. It would perhaps be oversimplifying the situation to say that the essential difference in the political attitudes of conservatives and liberals lay in their differing views on this question. And yet such a statement would contain a large element of truth. As Colden had pointed out, English history showed repeated changes in the balance. The eighteenth century appeared on the surface to be a period of equilibrium, but forces were stirring underneath which threatened the stability of the constitution. Which of these forces constituted the real danger for the future was uncertain. But the conservatives, at least, were certain that they knew.

As might be expected, American conservatives of the late colonial period contributed nothing new to the realm of political philosophy. Their ideas were circumscribed within the frame of the British constitution; their theories were derived originally from British experience; they reflected the attitudes of British writers. They believed in that constitution and in the principles upon which it was based. They might differ among themselves on the speculative question of the origin of government, but whether they accepted with the majority the doctrine of compact and consent, or denied it with Boucher and the extreme Tories, they agreed that the British constitution as they knew it was the perfect blending of the three elements of power. So long as the Americans followed the British model, keeping all three forces in nice adjustment, then their colonial governments would be sound and true. Schemers and demagogues might try to force a change, but men of wisdom and foresight should hold firm. If loyal men succeeded, if America were kept faithful to the past, then the colonies would grow in peace and prosperity under the leadership of the parent state. Then, like dutiful children, the colonies would wax strong and comely in the likeness of their glorious British mother.

THE TORY MIND

One of the many possible interpretations of the history of Western civilization is that it has been a long-continued conflict, or a succession of conflicts, between the forces of liberalism and the forces of conservatism. On the one side, there have been men and interests anxious to promote change in the character of institutions and the relationship of individuals and groups. They wish to keep society as much as possible in harmony with inevitable changes in the environment, with man's understanding and mastery of that environment, and with new developments in the realm of ideas. Sometimes they seek to bring about change simply in the interest of a particular class or group. On the other side, there have been those who have resisted such efforts at change, either because they do not admit the compelling force of external circumstance, because they doubt the effectiveness of the proposed remedies, or because they believe the changes will adversely affect the interests of themselves or their section of society. Much of the time the struggle between the representatives of these two points of view goes on quietly and with little surface disturbance. Once in a while, however, the conflict becomes acute, the issues seem to become more immediate, and the struggle between the contending forces comes out clearly into the open. Then there is likely to take place one of those great crises which we call revolutions, such as from time to time have punctuated the history of Western civilization.

The first such great crisis in the New World was the episode known as the American Revolution. When we use that term intelligently we mean by it something more than we do by the phrase "the War of Independence." The Revolution had its military phase, of course, but as a great movement it began long before the engagements at Lexington and Concord. As a contest between contending forces, it involved ideas and attitudes quite as much as it did armies and fighting ships. It was a revolt of colonies against the parent state, but it was also a civil conflict among fellow Americans who found themselves unable to agree on the solution of problems common to them all. In its outcome it did far more than establish the political independence of the thirteen United Colonies; it marked an initial victory for certain principles in the economic and social, as well as the political, organization of America, principles which have gained currency and strength until now we accept them as an essential part of the American way of life.

I have said that the Revolution was in part a civil conflict between fellow Americans who disagreed on the solution of some of their current problems. There were those who were willing from the start to use extreme measures to resist the decisions of the home government. There were others who objected to the policies of the ministry but counseled moderation and were drawn in to support the radicals only when the course of events seemed to leave them no other choice. There were still others — and these constituted a very large proportion of the total population — who wanted to take no part in the controversy, one way or the other, and hoped only to be left alone to pursue their own lives in peace and quiet. And lastly there was a substantial minority who in the end took sides with the British against their fellow colonials. These last were, in general, the men of conservative temperament in whom we are chiefly interested here.

Colonial conservatives might — as most of them actually did — believe that Britain was pursuing a mistaken policy in beginning to tax the colonies by act of Parliament. Here was an innovation, on principle quite as distressing to a colonial conservative as to a radical. But when the reaction to the parliamentary and ministerial measures went beyond the stage of respectful protest and led to civil disobedience and violence, some of the colonials drew back. When civil disobedience was followed by armed resistance, and then by a declaration of independence, and these were accompanied by an internal revolution in the institutions of colonial society itself, many Americans found themselves supporting the mother country. Not only was Britain the rightful claimant to their allegiance, but she was also the only agency that could be relied on to restore society to its proper foundations. Therefore, they sided with Great Britain. By contemporary Americans such men were bitterly called "Tories"; by their proud descendants in Canada and elsewhere and by a more understanding generation of Americans today they are more often referred to as "Loyalists."

A good deal of effort has been made at one time or another to find out just who were the Loyalists of the Revolution. Much has been written about individuals among them and about the treatment, or mistreatment, they received. But comparatively little has been said on the more fundamental question of *why* certain men were Loyalists. There has been comparatively little inquiry into the nature of the Tory mind and into the reasons for the Loyalist attitude to the great public questions of the day. These are problems that deserve attention.

The Loyalists were, above all others, the prime examples of the colonial conservative. In the Introduction to these lectures I defined conservatism as an attitude of mind that tends to promote resistance to change in one or another aspect of social relationships. The Revolutionary Era was certainly that period in eighteenth-century America in which change was most active and most far-reaching. Inevitably, therefore, it provided the greatest opportunity not only for the advancing of liberal or radical views but also for the expression of a conservative attitude.

In the course of our discussion we have seen how a relatively small group of privileged and largely related families in colonial America controlled an unduly large share of political power and have considered some of the economic groups among which conservatism was most apparent. Then we examined conservatism as it found expression in the religious, educational, and social life of the colonies, and analyzed the political theories of passive obedience, nonresistance, and balanced government expounded by spokesmen of conservative thought. Thus we have laid the foundation, in broad outline at least, for an understanding of conservatism as it expressed itself in word and in action in the greatest crisis of the whole colonial period.

In many cases, it is clear, men sided with the British government because it seemed to their personal advantage to do so. Such motives were especially obvious among members of the ruling class and particularly among royal or proprietary officeholders. These men had a vested interest, partly economic and partly social and psychological, in the maintenance of political leadership and in the prestige as well as the material rewards that went with public office. In large measure (although with many individual exceptions) direction and control of the revolutionary movement, which was originally in the hands of the accustomed political spokesmen, tended to pass in the course of time to men of little or no previous distinction or political importance. Their assumption of leadership, as well as the tactics they employed, alienated many a colonial notable who was not accustomed to seeing political power exercised by members of what he called the "mob." In this connection I have tried as one test case to discover just what proportion of the members of royal and proprietary councils at the outbreak of the war ought to be classed as Loyalists, either moderate or extreme. There did not prove to be enough accurate information to permit an exact statistical statement, but it would appear from the available evidence that from one half to two thirds of the councilors either openly espoused the British cause or were placed on parole by the Whigs as disaffected persons.

A large proportion of the administrative officers took the British side. Their action is easily understandable. Many were British-born and lived in America only because their jobs were here. Practically all stood to lose their salaries if the colonies became independent. William Eddis, royal surveyor of the customs and proprietary commissioner of the loan office in Maryland, expressed well the attitude of his fellow officeholders when he wrote soon after the Declaration of Independence: "I wish well to America — it is my duty — my inclination so to do — but I cannot — I will not — consent to act in direct opposition to my oath of allegiance and my deliberate opinion. Rather than submit to a conduct so base, so inconsistent with my principles, I will give up all — embrace ruin! — and trust to the protecting care of Providence for the future disposition of me and mine."[1]

Self-interest also played a part in determining the attitude of many of the great landowners and merchants. They were the leading men of property in the colonies with the most to lose from an upheaval in the orderly processes of society as it was constituted. These were the classes of men who, over the years, had tended to show the most consistent conservatism on other issues that challenged their economic or political leadership. It is not surprising, therefore, that from these groups there should emerge a large proportion of men who resisted the changes in society and the attack upon their control which the revolutionary movement threatened to produce.

Among such men, the position and attitude of the colonial

[1] Eddis, *Letters from America*, p. 217.

merchants has received much scholarly attention.[2] In the early stages of the dispute with Britain many of these men were active leaders in the opposition to the mother country. It was the merchants themselves who brought about the first nonimportation agreements. Several of them, later distinguished as Loyalists, were elected to the Stamp Act Congress. It took time for these men to see that they had started something they could not stop and finally could not even control. At first they apparently did not object greatly to the somewhat boisterous popular demonstrations against British acts. As Carl Becker has effectively put it, "a little rioting was well enough, so long as it was directed to the one end of bringing the English government to terms. But when the destruction of property began to be relished for its own sake by those who had no property and the cry of liberty came loudest from those who were without political privilege, it was time to call a halt. These men might not cease their shouting when purely British restrictions were removed."[3] Many a man who joined heartily in the first steps of organized protest came to regret his acts. Many an essentially conservative colonial discovered to his dismay that he had unwittingly cast himself in the role of Pandora.

Some merchants were more cautious from the start. John Watts, a leading businessman of New York, for example, objected to the Stamp Act but wrote a friend in November 1765 that he believed no prudent man should meddle with the question of parliamentary taxation except among friends as a mere matter of speculation. "The less is said on the subject," he added,

---

[2] The outstanding work is, of course, Arthur M. Schlesinger's *The Colonial Merchants and the American Revolution*. Also important are Charles M. Andrews, "The Boston Merchants and the Non-Importation Movement," *Publications* of the Colonial Society of Massachusetts, XIX (Boston, 1918), 159–259; and Virginia D. Harrington, *The New York Merchant on the Eve of the Revolution*.

[3] Becker, *Political Parties*, p. 31.

"the better on this side; 'tis too delicate if not presumptuous."[4]
There were others who felt as Watts did and later could pride
themselves on their consistent behavior. Whether a merchant
was an active instigator of nonimportation agreements or one
who refused to take any steps in the face of injurious British
legislation, he was likely before long to feel that the chief threat
to his prosperity and to the principle of property rights came
not from the British Parliament but from the colonial radicals.
With the exception of those merchants who engaged largely in
smuggling, their class depended for their business chiefly on the
orderly conduct of overseas trade. Economic boycott was an
effective but a highly expensive weapon; experience with it led
many merchants to regret their public-spirited adherence to the
nonimportation agreements.

What in many cases was quite as important as the immediate
financial loss which the merchants suffered in the dispute was
the changed attitude of the lower classes. In this matter the other
men of property, especially the landed gentry in the North,
joined the merchants. The "vulgar" had found a new sport, the
destruction of property. A man like John Watts might deplore
the burning of Lieutenant Governor Colden's coach by the
Stamp Act rioters, but he would not be too upset about it, for
he detested Colden personally. But when, nearly five years later,
a midnight mob seized and burned some goods which the New
York merchants' Committee of Inspection had sequestered for
violation of the nonimportation agreement, such merchants as
Isaac Low, head of the committee, were outraged. He and his
fellow committeemen denounced the act as "a high insult" to
themselves and the city and branded the perpetrators as "lawless
ruffians."[5] And when in 1773 the "Indians" of Boston dumped

---

[4] *Letter Book of John Watts*, p. 400.
[5] Schlesinger, *Colonial Merchants and the American Revolution*, p.
190.

£15,000 worth of tea into the harbor, and the next year citizens of Maryland publicly burned the tea ship "Peggy Stewart," owned by Annapolis merchants, it became perfectly clear to men of wealth and standing that the sacred right of property was under attack. Men of this class came to believe that it had been a mistake to sanction agitation against authority in the first place. Now authority had to be supported if their own property were to be safeguarded. In such terms many men began to see the issues of the times and, accordingly, chose to uphold the Crown in their own self-interest.

So far we have been considering only those special groups of Americans for whom economic self-interest was an important and obvious motive in support of a Loyalist position. Much has been said, by historians and by nonhistorians alike, about the importance of economic motives in the determination of historical events. I, for one, should certainly agree that material forces have had and still do have a large share in the shaping of society and in the actions of human beings. Man does not live in an economic vacuum. At the same time, I firmly believe that a purely materialistic interpretation of history is inadequate and untenable. Man does not live in a vacuum, but neither could he live for long if he were to breathe pure oxygen alone. A strictly economic interpretation of history is at best only a partial interpretation.

Loyalism in the Revolutionary period, while it had for many men an economic basis, cannot be explained wholly on materialistic grounds, nor can the Loyalists be fully classified into economic groups. Support of the British government was to be found in every section, every calling, and every class. A lowly tenant farmer of New York colony or an insignificant shopkeeper of a North Carolina village could be just as faithful to the Crown as the Reverend Jonathan Boucher of Maryland or His Excellency, Governor Thomas Hutchinson of Massachusetts. Loyalism was not only a consequence of social or economic position; it was quite as much the result of an attitude of mind.

That attitude of mind was not identical among all supporters of the Crown, but there were enough points of general similarity to justify us in trying to identify some of the chief characteristics and attitudes of what we may call the Tory mind. First and foremost I should put what can be most simply described as the conservative temperament.

Psychologists do not seem able to agree on an explanation of why some men should generally support new ideas and social innovations while others tend to resist changes in conventional attitudes and in the structure of society. Factors of personality, of individual conditioning, of subconscious motivation, and of sheer human inertia doubtless all play their part, even if no simple or universally acceptable theory can be advanced as yet to explain these differences in men's responses to social change. In the course of these lectures we have seen how, in a variety of situations and on a number of important issues, a proportion of the colonists reacted against threatened changes in the patterns of American life, even when their own economic interest was not directly involved. These were the men of conservative temperament. If we have gained any insight into their attitudes throughout the pre-Revolutionary century, we have acquired a basis for understanding why men of like temperament refused to support the even greater changes implicit in the Revolution itself. Intangible and hard to define though it may be, this trait of personality which I have called the conservative temperament is, I believe, the most important single characteristic of the Tory mind.

A second factor conditioning the minds and attitudes of many Loyalists was that of religion — more specifically of religious belief and religious affiliation. This point is obviously important in connection with those whose religious beliefs included the principle of pacifism, notably the Quakers and members of several of the German sects. We have mentioned already the protest of the Quaker leaders at the closing of Philadelphia business houses in sympathy with the inhabitants of Boston when the Port Act went into effect. Even that demonstration, these Friends said, violated their religious principles.[6] The belief in submission to constituted authority became even more important in determining the Quaker position when independence became the central issue. Within ten days after Tom Paine's *Common Sense* appeared on the streets of Philadelphia, the Friends' convention issued an address "to the people in general." After dilating upon the benefits of the British connection, the address laid down the fundamental principle that "the setting up and putting down [of] kings and government is God's peculiar prerogative, for causes best known to Himself, and it is not our business to have any hand or contrivance therein."[7] With such expressions of belief coming from the leaders of the Quaker community, it is not surprising that, however much they might deplore the measures of the British government, a large proportion of the Friends found that they could not in conscience withdraw their loyalty and obedience to the established government.

While pacifism in the general sense was not a religious principle of the Church of England, we have already seen how most

[6] See above, p. 128. In October 1774 the epistle of the Philadelphia Yearly Meeting had urged all Friends to avoid purchasing any smuggled goods, so that "we may not be in any way instrumental in countenancing or promoting the iniquity, false swearing, and violence which are the common consequences of an unlawful and clandestine trade. May we . . . . by this and every other part of our conduct, give a public testimony of our sincere desire that we may submit to the just administration of the laws, agreeable to our Christian principles." *Rivington's New-York Gazetteer*, October 27, 1774, No. 80.

[7] Lincoln, *Revolutionary Movement in Pennsylvania*, pp. 238–39.

of the Anglican clergy preached nonresistance and civil obedience as an important part of the beliefs of their denomination.[8] While discussing the established churches in the colonies we observed, also, the special place which the Anglican Communion enjoyed and the sense of connection with the mother country and its institutions which membership in that religious body brought to many of its adherents, especially in the North.[9] For some of the clergy, it is true, loyalism may have seemed to be a matter of bread and butter, but for the greater part of them it was the result of a sincere conviction that resistance to established authority was morally wrong and that it was their Christian duty to support the home government in the existing crisis. As the Anglican ministers of New York and New Jersey declared in 1771, "the members of the National Church are from principle and inclination firmly attached to the Constitution. From them it must ever derive its surest support."[10] To the steadfastness of many of the Anglican clergy one of their number later paid tribute by applying to them these lines from *Paradise Lost*:

> Among the faithless, faithful chiefly they—
> Among innumerable false, unmov'd,
> Unshaken, unseduc'd, unterrified,
> Their *loyalty* they kept, their love, their zeal:
> Nor number, nor example, with them wrought,
> To swerve from truth, or change their constant mind.[11]

To many Americans, notably among the Congregational and Presbyterian ministers, religious principles seemed to justify

[8] See above, pp. 74–75, 128–30.

[9] See above, pp. 70–74.

[10] Cross, *Anglican Episcopate*, p. 255, quoting from *New Jersey Archives*, X, 309–13.

[11] Boucher, *American Revolution*, p. xlix n., quoting from *Paradise Lost*, Bk. V, ll. 897–902. Boucher altered the text slightly, changed the pronouns from singular to plural, and added the italics.

and even perhaps actively to encourage participation in the Revolutionary movement.[12] To some men of other denominations, however, and especially to many Quakers, Mennonites, and Anglicans, a sincere obedience to the teachings of the faith could lead, at whatever cost, only to obedience to constituted authority and loyalty to the Crown.

A point of importance to an understanding to the Tory mind as it exhibited itself in the Revolutionary conflict is that loyalism was in many cases a matter of slow development. There were a few, but only a few, colonists who openly approved the British policy from the time of the Stamp Act. Perhaps the most extreme statement of an early ultraconservative view came from an anonymous writer in New Jersey in 1765. On the right of Parliament to tax the colonies he was as firm as Grenville himself. "Does not all history inform us," he asked, "that colonies were always in absolute dependence on the mother state, and only received her commands?" The author flatly denied that the Americans' ancestors had brought with them all the privileges of Englishmen. Particularly they did not bring liberty, he said, for liberty and property always go together. The first settlers were generally very poor and so brought little or no property with them. Therefore they could not then bring liberty, and if they had no liberty their descendants obviously had not inherited it. The colonial charters were merely "a parcel of old musty papers" in which Parliament had never concurred and which were now obsolete. "How then," he asked, "can the Parliament be bound by them or have their hands tied up by what the Crown did a hundred years ago?" With such words and with many more to the same effect spoke the earliest and most

[12] Discussions of this matter may be found in: Alice M. Baldwin, *The New England Clergy and the American Revolution;* and Leonard J. Kramer, "The Political Ethics of the American Presbyterian Clergy in the Eighteenth Century" (unpublished dissertation in the Yale University Library).

extreme ultraconservative I have found among those who professed to be actual Americans.[13]

Such an attitude was not characteristic of the Tory mind in general in 1765. In most cases strict loyalism grew slowly. Just as a desire for complete independence came only gradually to all but a very few extremists on the other side, so a decision to side finally and fully with Great Britain was reached, in the case of most Loyalists, only after the dispute began to reach its climax.

Almost every colonist of English ancestry asserted proudly his claim to the rights and liberties of an Englishman, and nearly everyone, including most of those who later became known as the stanchest Loyalists, believed that Parliament had been far from wise in its legislation of 1764 and 1765. Thomas Hutchinson declared later that he had not approved the Stamp Act at the time of its passage, though as a servant of the Crown he thought himself bound "to discountenance the violent opposition made to the act, as it led to the denial of [Parliament's] authority in all cases whatsoever."[14] Many thoroughgoing conservatives quite openly expressed their objections to the parliamentary measures, on grounds of both principle and expediency, and modified their position only when they decided that the public opposition was producing worse evils than would the acts themselves. In many cases it was the radicals' increasing resort to violence that won these men over to the British side.

Timothy Ruggles, chief justice of Massachusetts, was a comparatively early convert. He was elected president of the Stamp Act Congress in 1765 but would not sign the petitions that body drew up and was later reported to have threatened to jail every-

---

[13] The General Advertiser for the New-York Thursday's Gazette, October 10, 1765 (a postscript sheet to The New-York Gazette or the Weekly Postboy, No. 1188.

[14] Hutchinson, Diary and Letters, II, 57–58.

one who signed the nonimportation agreement of 1774. Isaac Low, the New York merchant, was likewise a delegate to the Stamp Act Congress. In 1768 he headed the New York Committee of Inspection to enforce the nonimportation agreement of that year, and in 1774 was a member of the First Continental Congress and signed the Association. But he was already swinging over to a moderate position, and when the British occupied the city in 1776 he remained there, becoming president of the Chamber of Commerce under British auspices in 1779. When the royal troops evacuated the city at the end of the war he moved to England. Joseph Galloway, of Pennsylvania, as is well known, was a delegate to the First Continental Congress chiefly interested in working out a compromise solution of the constitutional issue. He refused election to the Second Congress and later fled to Howe's army, becoming civil administrator of Philadelphia during the British occupation and then going to England where he became the spokesman for the exiled Loyalists. Jacob Duché, native-born Anglican clergyman of Philadelphia, to give a final example, was such a zealot in the cause of "liberty" as to win for himself both the denunciations of his fellow minister, Boucher, and appointment by the Continental Congress as its chaplain. But the Declaration of Independence changed his views; he urged its recall and was in turn denounced as a traitor by the Americans. He left for England in 1777, where he became, almost symbolically in his lonely exile, chaplain of an orphan asylum.[15]

The slow crystallization of loyalism in the minds of many individuals suggests another characteristic in the thinking of many men of that day. It is easy for us to set in contrast the extremists of both sides—Samuel Adams against Thomas Hutchinson, for example—as if all men who wrote or spoke

[15] There are useful sketches of all four of these men in the *Dictionary of American Biography*.

in those days could be simply classified as "Patriots" or as "Tories." But there were many who cannot easily be so listed and who, whether or not they finally maintained their loyalty to the king, should properly be classed as "Moderates." A considerable proportion of those who earned the enmity of the American radicals did so in the first instance because they advocated moderation in the championing of American rights. With many who later became out-and-out Loyalists, a first and a preferred position was one of moderation and of protest against extremism of word or action.

As time passed and parliamentary measures brought continued forceful opposition in America, men of conservative temper again and again expressed their hope that resistance and retaliation would not be carried to extremes. In December 1773, after the passage of the Tea Act, one who signed himself "A Farmer" put the case for moderation in a public letter to the inhabitants of the city and colony of New York. He began with the proposition, which he hoped would be readily granted, that whoever wished well to the interests of Great Britain and America and really wanted to have the revenue act repealed would favor the most lenient measures. "Violence in opposition to government," he affirmed, "should ever be kept aloof and held as the *dernier resort*," and whoever promoted violence, "save in the last extremity," should be suspected as an enemy of the cause he appeared to espouse. In the present case, Parliament might in time be persuaded to repeal the act, "but they will *never be braved into it*."[16] From many points of view the "Farmer's" advice was good, as many men on both sides would

---

[16] *Rivington's New-York Gazetteer*, December 2, 1773, No. 33. In his introductory essay to the Reverend Samuel Seabury's *Letters of a Westchester Farmer* (*1774-1775*) (Publications of the Westchester County Historical Society, VII, White Plains, 1930), Clarence H. Vance suggests the possibility that this letter was written by Seabury as the first of a series intended for Rivington's paper but never continued.

agree; there is no question but that his prophecy about the attitude of Parliament proved correct. Just two weeks after his letter appeared in New York a group of extremists in Boston determined on a drastic measure regarding the tea which had reached that port. Certainly their action did not "brave" Parliament into a repeal of the act; on the contrary, the retaliation which the Tea Party provoked from England brought closer than ever before those extremes of violence that the moderates had hoped so earnestly to prevent.

The time when men could still cling to such hopes of moderation was rapidly drawing to a close. Before long the extremists of both sides made the ultimate appeal to force, and those who had sought a middle course were asked to choose which side they would support. Some men like William Samuel Johnson of Connecticut or James Duane of New York finally sided with the revolting colonists; others like James Galloway went over to the British; still others tried to remain neutral.

In revolution there is little room for neutrality. Applying the theory that "those who are not for us are against us," most of the American revolutionaries tended to class the moderate conservatives who would not join them as Tories at heart. Many of these moderates were made to suffer, both then and later, as if they were avowedly in the hostile camp. Men of this moderate temper appear in nearly every time of stress. Essentially, they are conservatives, but conservatives cursed with an ability to see that there are two sides to an issue, and unable or unwilling to choose finally and irrevocably with which side they will cast their fortunes. No examination of the men who failed to join the American cause in the Revolution is adequate which fails to take into account the position of those moderates who preferred to remain neutral and who in many cases were driven into active loyalism only by the hostility of their uncomprehending and impatient fellow colonists.

Another fact which we must recognize if we are to understand the Tory mind is that, in spite of time and distance, many Americans still had a deep attachment to Great Britain and nearly all had a sincere admiration for the British constitution. England was the mother country for a large proportion of the colonists, and even if they were several generations removed from English birth they still took pride in being Englishmen. Observers in both North and South reported throughout the eighteenth century that people of means and culture reproduced as far as they could English manners, dress, and conversation, affecting in all things to be as much English as possible. They bought or copied English clothes, read English books, followed English politics, and looked across to England as the source and center of their cultural life. Over and over the records show that even colonists who had never been in Great Britain wrote and spoke of it as "home."

This sentimental attachment to the mother country was reinforced by a positive belief in the real value and importance of the British connection and in the merits of the British constitution. Many men would agree with "Rusticus," who wrote early in 1775 that the "peace and security" the colonists had enjoyed before 1764 under the British connection "must make us look back with regret to those happy days whose loss we mourn and which every rational man must consider as the golden age of America."[17] John Randolph of Virginia pointed out at about the same time that "a more pleasing and natural connection never subsisted between any different bodies of men" than had, until lately, existed between Great Britain and her colonies. The inhabitants of both were allied by blood and by their mutual trade and commerce. In manners, religion, language, and laws there were only the minor differences occasioned by local

[17] *Dunlap's Pennsylvania Packet, or, the General Advertiser,* January 2, 1775, No. 167.

circumstances. "Whilst we remain tied together by one friendly and common band," said Randolph, "we can preserve our religion and property from violation and bid defiance to all the hostile powers on earth; but if this ligament be burst assunder, our strength will be weakened and our security at an end."[18]

Some Loyalists, looking back at the course of events over several generations and seeing how rapidly America had been growing in population and strength, recognized that independence was bound to come sooner or later. The colonies were developing too fast to be kept indefinitely in a subordinate position. Even the writer who had referred yearningly to the earlier "golden age of America" spoke also of "that future independency which, in the course of human affairs, these colonies must arrive at."[19] Yet, like all true conservatives when confronted by the inevitability of change, these men wanted to put it off as long as possible. Separation from the mother country might ultimately be inevitable, but the time, they thought, had not yet come. There were still avenues of accommodation to be explored before America plunged down the bloody path of civil war to total independence. Such was the burden of many a plea, especially in Philadelphia after the publication of Tom Paine's *Common Sense*. Thus one newspaper writer urged that independence ought to be a last resort only. "Let us not yet lose sight," he begged, "of the primary object of the dispute, namely, a safe, honorable, and lasting reconciliation with Great Britain." Until this proved impossible no steps toward separation would be warranted.[20] Another writer, who admitted "that nature must, at last, have its course and a total separation take place between

---

[18] [Randolph], *Considerations on the Present State of Virginia*, p. 23.

[19] *Dunlap's Pennsylvania Packet, or, the General Advertiser*, January 2, 1775, No. 167. He added, however, that independence "cannot for our true interest be too long delayed."

[20] *The Pennsylvania Gazette*, February 28, 1776, No. 2462.

the New and the Old World," argued that at that moment —
the spring of 1776 — there were only two grand questions: *"Is
a change necessary*, and *Is this the time for it?"* To both these
questions he would answer with a resounding "No." Like many
another conservative before and since, he could not accept the
idea that the time for the inevitable change had yet come.[21]

Another characteristic of the Tory mind was caution. The
conservative naturally wants to know to what he is committing
himself when he agrees to a course of action. He does not like
to sign blank checks. One of the troubles with the proposal for
independence was that it left the future so dark and uncertain.
Would it bring such benefits and happiness as its advocates insisted? Or would it bring unknown loss and suffering instead?
Could it offer anything to compensate for the known advantages of colonial status? Looking into the future of an independent America, conservatives could read no satisfactory answers
to these questions. Some thought they could guess what independence would bring and shuddered at the thought. Colonel
Landon Carter, one of the last of the great Virginia planters to
climb off the fence on the American side, could see only the rise
of arbitrary power, oppression, and tyranny within America.[22]
One Philadelphia writer assured his readers that the advocates
of independence were trying to hurry them "into a scene of
anarchy." But the worst was that no one really knew what
might follow independence. As he went on to point out, the
radicals' "scheme of independence is visionary; they know not
themselves what they mean by it." Separation was a "leap in the
dark."[23] One of the Loyalists who tried to answer *Common*

[21] *Dunlap's Pennsylvania Packet, or, the General Advertiser*, April 29,
1776, No. 236, postscript.

[22] Entries of March 29, May 23, May 29, and June 14, 1776, "Diary of
Colonel Landon Carter," *William and Mary Quarterly*, 1st Series, XVI
(April 1908), 258; XVIII (July 1909), 38–39, 43–44, 176–77.

[23] *The Pennsylvania Gazette*, May 1, 1776, No. 2471.

Sense argued that reconciliation would restore a known state of happiness. Trade, agriculture, and industry would flourish as before. "Pennsylvania has much to lose in this contest and much to hope from a proper settlement of it." The colony had long flourished under its charter government. "What may be the consequences of another form we cannot pronounce with certainty; but this we know, that it is a road we have not traveled, and may be worse than it is described."[24] And so like the good conservatives they were, many of the Tories, coming to the parting of the ways, turned aside from the dark and unknown path marked "Independence," and marched firmly down the familiar way of "Loyalty."

Part of the uncertainty over the future of an independent America came directly out of the experience of the years that just preceded the outbreak of warfare. Those years did little to bring assurance that Americans would of their own volition re-establish a government of decency and order. We have already given attention to the attitude of the men of great wealth to the radicals' disregard of property rights. Many others shared this feeling without apparent regard to the extent of their personal fortunes. And if to the actual destruction of merchants' ships and goods be added the lootings of houses like Thomas Hutchinson's, the tarrings and featherings, the intimidation of officials, the general rioting and mob rule, the setting up of extralegal committees and associations, the "demagoguery" of the radical leaders, and the enfranchisement of the propertyless common people, then the prospect that a government of law and wisdom could be established in America seemed remote indeed.

From the very start of the troubles there were men to denounce the resort to violence. Perhaps none put the issue on a

[24] *Dunlap's Pennsylvania Packet, or, the General Advertiser*, March 25, 1776, No. 231; *The Pennsylvania Gazette*, March 27, 1776, No. 2466.

higher plane than did "A Colonist" of New York. Writing in that same troubled autumn of 1765, he pointed out that "the late newspapers have been filled with accounts of mobs, riots, burning in effigy, and resignations of officers, which have been read with pleasure by too many." The writer, on the other hand, was filled only with melancholy when he "looked forward and considered the consequences of such proceedings." The inhabitants of America had the undoubted right to seek redress for the invasion of their rights, "but let us assert our liberties or demand the repeal of a law like honest freemen; let us not stain our characters by entering into riots we are ashamed of." "Do not we blush," he asked, "when we hear that under the pretense of asserting and maintaining the cause of liberty, robbery, and the most atrocious crimes have been committed," and men have joined in mobs, sometimes for personal revenge, sometimes out of avarice, and sometimes to serve their personal ambitions? No cool-thinking man could read with pleasure "that a fellow subject has had his house pulled down and been robbed of his furniture and money, because he has differed in opinion from us." Freedom of speech, he went on, was an essential part of liberty, "but those destroy all freedom and become lawless tyrants, who take the liberty to ruin a fellow citizen for speaking his mind and advising his countrymen."[25] Thus in the opinion of this colonist, the resort to extralegal action was a threat not only to the property of individual Americans but to one of their fundamental freedoms as well—freedom of speech. Men who understood such a threat as this might well draw back from associating themselves with the party that permitted it.

As the period of agitation went on and the liberties of individuals were more and more invaded, not only by riotous mobs,

[25] *The General Advertiser for the New-York Thursday's Gazette,* October 10, 1765 (a postscript sheet to *The New-York Gazette or the Weekly Postboy,* No. 1188).

but also by committees and tribunals unauthorized by law, some men became more and more concerned for the future. The American people seemed to them to give little promise of being able to create a political structure that "honest men" could respect. Those who believed in a government well balanced between the monarchical, the aristocratic, and the democratic elements felt that the balance had already been badly upset. If independence were to be achieved, matters were likely to get worse rather than better. Only by a restoration of British authority was there any hope that the three essential elements of government could be brought back to their true and historic equilibrium.

We have now enumerated the chief characteristics of the Tory mind in the era of the American Revolution. There were individual and group differences among the Loyalists and, for many of them, such as officeholders, owners of large property, and merchants, questions of economic self-interest played a significant part. Having first recognized these facts, we must understand the following eight points if we are to understand the men who finally sided with the British in the great dispute: First, they were men of an essentially conservative temperament, disposed from the start to resist innovation and to support the old and the familiar. Second, many though not all of them held the conviction, based usually on religious belief and church affiliation, that, whatever the merits of the dispute, resistance to constituted authority and to the British government was morally wrong. Third, while a few sided with the ministry from the beginning, most Loyalists reached their final position only slowly and after much difficulty. One of the major factors that led many of them to make this decision was that they were alienated from the supporters of resistance by the continued use of violence and other forms of extreme action. Fourth, some men were really forced into out-and-out loyalism by the refusal of their fellow colonists to permit them to keep to a middle-of-the-road position. Fifth, there was a sentimental attachment to Britain, an admiration for the constitution, and a belief in the value of the British connection, all of which made men reluctant to break with the mother country. Sixth, we can recognize the very human tendency to procrastinate. While many conservatives admitted that eventually independence would be inevitable, they wanted to put off the evil day and so refused to admit that the time for such action had now arrived. Seventh, the Tory mind was cautious. Men were reluctant to accept an unknown future without guarantees that it would provide conditions at least as satisfactory as those they were giving up. Eighth and last, the Loyalist was pessimistic. He feared that the disturbed conditions of the Revolutionary period would be perpetuated if America gained her independence and that the new regime would raise the ignorant, disorderly element of society to a position of permanent and undesirable supremacy. He had little faith in the political capacity of the average American. These, I believe, were the essential features of Tory thinking. They all represent typically conservative attitudes. In displaying these characteristics during the great crisis the American Loyalist earned the right to be considered the culminating example of the colonial conservative.

Participation in revolution — except for those whose motives are most narrowly selfish — requires a special kind of imaginative courage, one compounded of a general bravery in the face of an uncertain future, faith in that future, a power to imagine vividly how it may be molded to a desired end, and an optimistic disregard of the possibilities of loss or of failure to attain the hoped-for goal. All great revolutionaries have had that sort of courage, whether or not the movements they led have, in the long perspective of history, been successful, or have sought ends to the real interest of humanity. The conservatives who have

opposed such revolutions—again apart from those whose motives have been primarily ones of self-interest—have seldom
been endowed with this sort of courage. Again and again they
have displayed a different group of virtues: a strong sense of the
values in the contemporary order of society that are in danger
of being lost, an imagination keen enough to see the possible
harm as well as the good in the changes proposed, and a personal
bravery in the face of suffering and persecution.

Thus it was with the sincere Loyalists of the American Revolution. They saw more clearly than did some of their opponents
the values inherent in their colonial past, in the tradition of
government by law which was theirs under the British constitution, and in the strength and external security afforded by the
British connection. They recognized the dangers threatening a
future state founded in violence and disorder by a group of
leaders many of whom were quite inexperienced in the art of
government. And when their turn came to suffer in their persons and in their property and even by banishment or death,
many of the Loyalists made the required sacrifice with a dignity
and fortitude worthy of the highest admiration. What they
lacked, what made them Loyalists rather than revolutionists,
was the other sort of courage and imagination. They saw the
dangers ahead rather than the noble possibilities. They did not
have the daring needed to strike for a better future even at the
risk of losing a present good. They lacked—many of them—a
sufficient faith in mankind, in common, American mankind, to
believe that out of disorder and violence, out of an inexperienced leadership and an undisciplined following, could come a
stable and intelligent body politic. They were Loyalists, in
short, because they had both the weakness and the strength of
all true conservatives.

Our examination of American conservatism in the hundred
years before the achievement of independence has now run its

course. I have tried to point out how early American conservatism expressed itself, to describe the major conservative groups and institutions, and to show how the conservatives reacted to some of the significant problems of their times. It is possible that in focusing attention on these features of colonial history I have given the impression that I consider the conservative forces in colonial life more important than those which led to change and development. That has not been my intention. The century before independence was anything but a static period in American life. Growth, expansion, change were of the very essence of the history of those years. It is, however, just because development and movement were so important and so striking that we are apt to forget the elements of constancy in the record and to overlook those men whose natures and attitudes led them to resist the forces of social change. My aim has been to bring this part of the picture for a moment under the historian's lens in order that the whole pattern may emerge in clearer, sharper outline.

In discussing the colonial conservative I have tried to keep the balance even — avoiding both undue praise and unjust condemnation. It is not, I believe, the historian's right or duty to pass judgment on the past in terms of the social or moral standards of his own day. An Olympian attitude is neither a profitable nor a dignified posture for a scholar to assume. It *is* the historian's duty to try to *understand* the past both for its own sake as a part of our human heritage and as a means toward understanding and intelligently dealing with the related problems of the present. It is in those terms that I have tried to consider the colonial conservative.

Those were formative years, years in which our forefathers were building a new society and what came to be a new nation in a new world. They were years in which new influences and new ideas were working upon old traditions and old attitudes, not wholly rejecting them and casting them aside, but modifying and transforming them, and together with them creating something distinctive and different, something we call American civilization. In this process the old and the traditional played their part, and the upholders of the old and the traditional — that is, the colonial conservatives — made their contribution to the result.

The function of the conservative in society is twofold, partly negative and partly positive. Negatively he acts as a brake upon the process of social change. It is a common observation that the most effective and most lasting changes in social institutions are apt to be those which come relatively slowly. Sudden changes, especially those which take place before the community as a whole has accepted the fundamental theories on which they rest, are often temporary and only partially successful. Those which come more slowly, after a period of preparation and of public education, are likely to become more permanent and essential parts of the society into which they are introduced. By resisting the process of change and by forcing its advocates to justify their ideas in the minds of a larger segment of the public, the conservative, therefore, often contributes unintentionally but no less effectively to the successful accomplishment of a long-range transformation.

But the conservative's service to society is not wholly negative. Few of us would be interested in history if we did not believe that man's past experience has produced many ideas and institutions that have continuing importance and usefulness for the present. Rash, impetuous, or visionary men, with theories of how the world may be transformed overnight into something much more nearly perfect than it is, sometimes need to be reminded of these values from the past. In the process of social change those members of society who conserve such values so that they may be woven into the pattern of the future perform an important service to later generations.

Thus it was with the conservatives of the colonial period in America. It was not they primarily who gave this nation its distinctive and special character, who introduced here the ideas of economic opportunity, religious liberty, and political freedom which we like to think are fundamental doctrines of the American faith. It was not they who developed the theories of social and political equality that have undermined, though without fully destroying, the aristocratic class system inherited from Europe. It was not they who gained us our independence. But it was the conservatives, more than any others, who were responsible for the perpetuation in a raw, new country of much that was best in the cultural heritage from the Old World. It was the essentially conservative great landowners and wealthy merchants, above all, who kept in contact with that culture during the formative years of our American beginnings and introduced here some of the books, the science, the architecture, and the art of gracious living that formed part of the European civilization of their day. It was the conservative spokesmen in the churches during the excitement of the Great Awakening who reminded the people that true religion ought not to be founded upon mere emotionalism but upon true faith and sincere obedience. It was the conservative political leaders who opposed the use of violence as an instrument of politics and worked to maintain here a government based on law and order. It was the colonial conservatives who, in some degree, slowed down the process of social change. Without them the physical separation from Europe, the frontier, and the new environment generally might well have led to the destruction of much that we hold important in our lives today. Without them new theories of human freedom and social organization might have been put into practice without proper testing and before they had proved their right to general acceptance. The relative stability and continued growth of American society owes much to the influence of the conservative leaders of the colonial and Revolutionary periods.

For these reasons they deserve at least the tribute of our understanding. Although in the course of time most of us have moved far away from the positions they took on many of the problems of their age, we can recognize that they played a significant part in the building of this nation. Conservatism in early American history, like conservatism throughout the human record, has made its own special contribution to the development of society.

INDEX